MAFIA III

THE RISE AND FALL OF Sal Marcano

MAFIA III

THE RISE AND FALL OF Sal Marcano

Written by Frank Tieri

Illustrated by Richard Pace

Colors by Peter Pantazis

INSIGHT COMICS

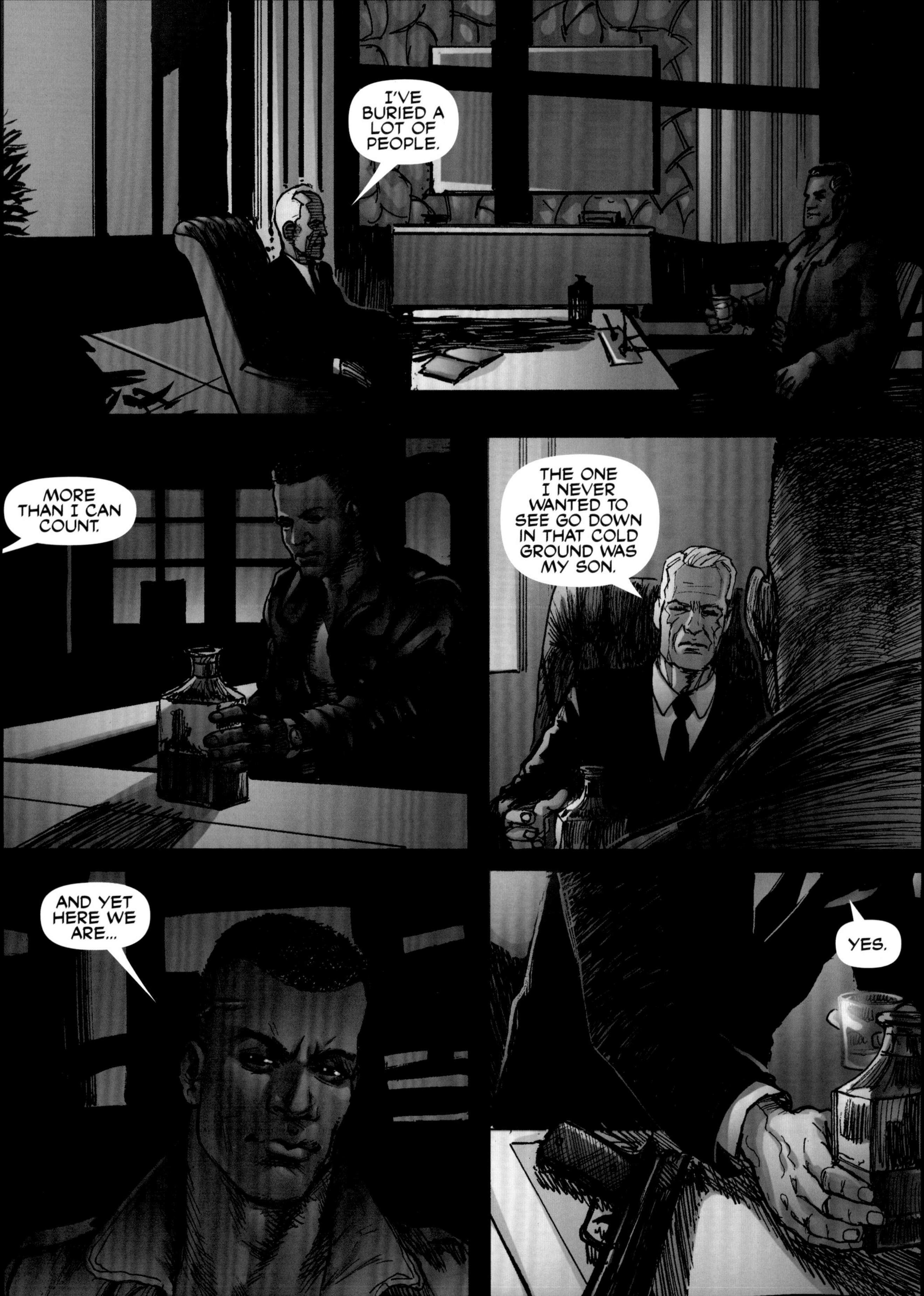
I'VE BURIED A LOT OF PEOPLE.
MORE THAN I CAN COUNT.
THE ONE I NEVER WANTED TO SEE GO DOWN IN THAT COLD GROUND WAS MY SON.
AND YET HERE WE ARE...
YES.

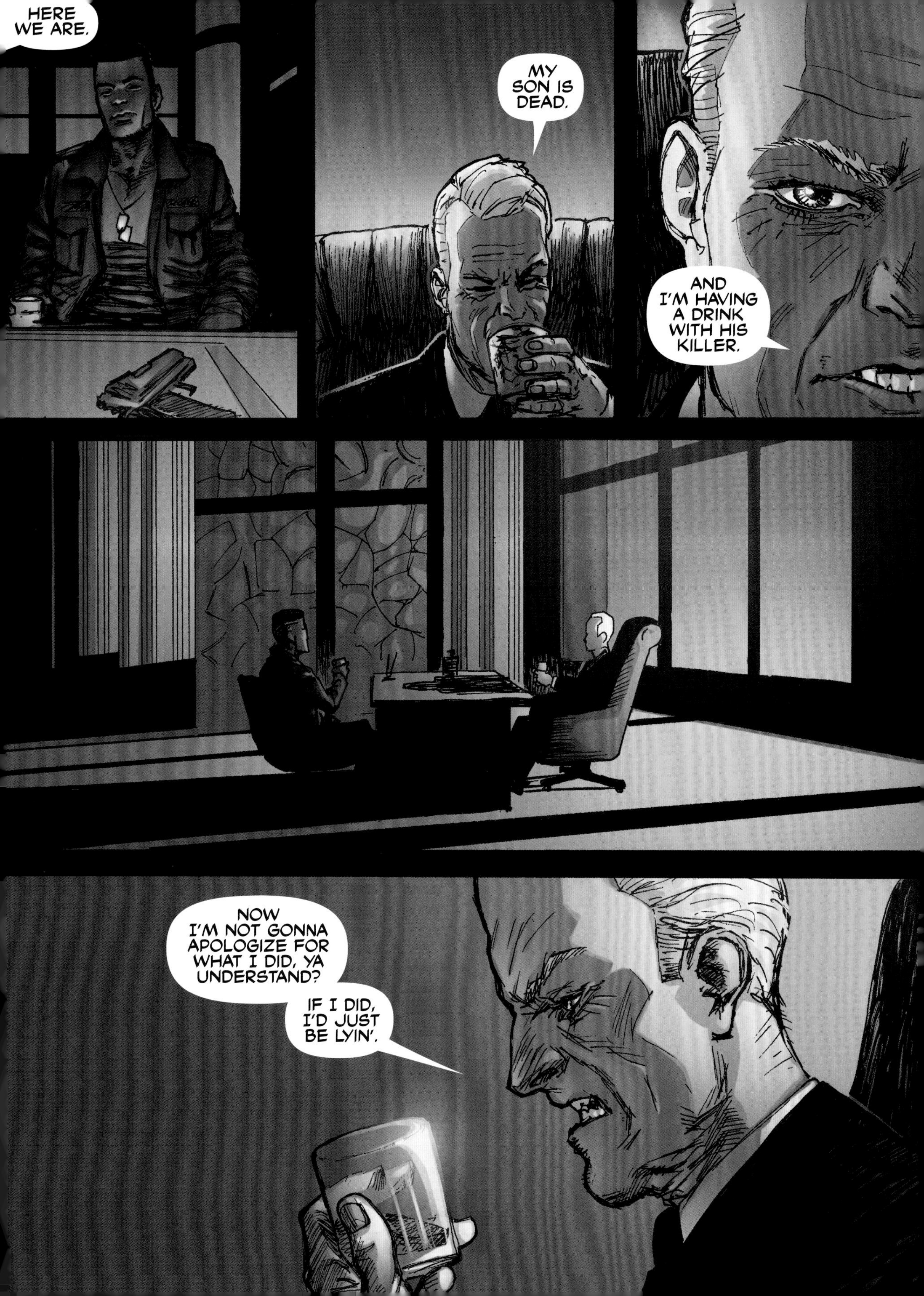
HERE WE ARE.
MY SON IS DEAD.
AND I'M HAVING A DRINK WITH HIS KILLER.
NOW I'M NOT GONNA APOLOGIZE FOR WHAT I DID, YA UNDERSTAND?
IF I DID, I'D JUST BE LYIN'.

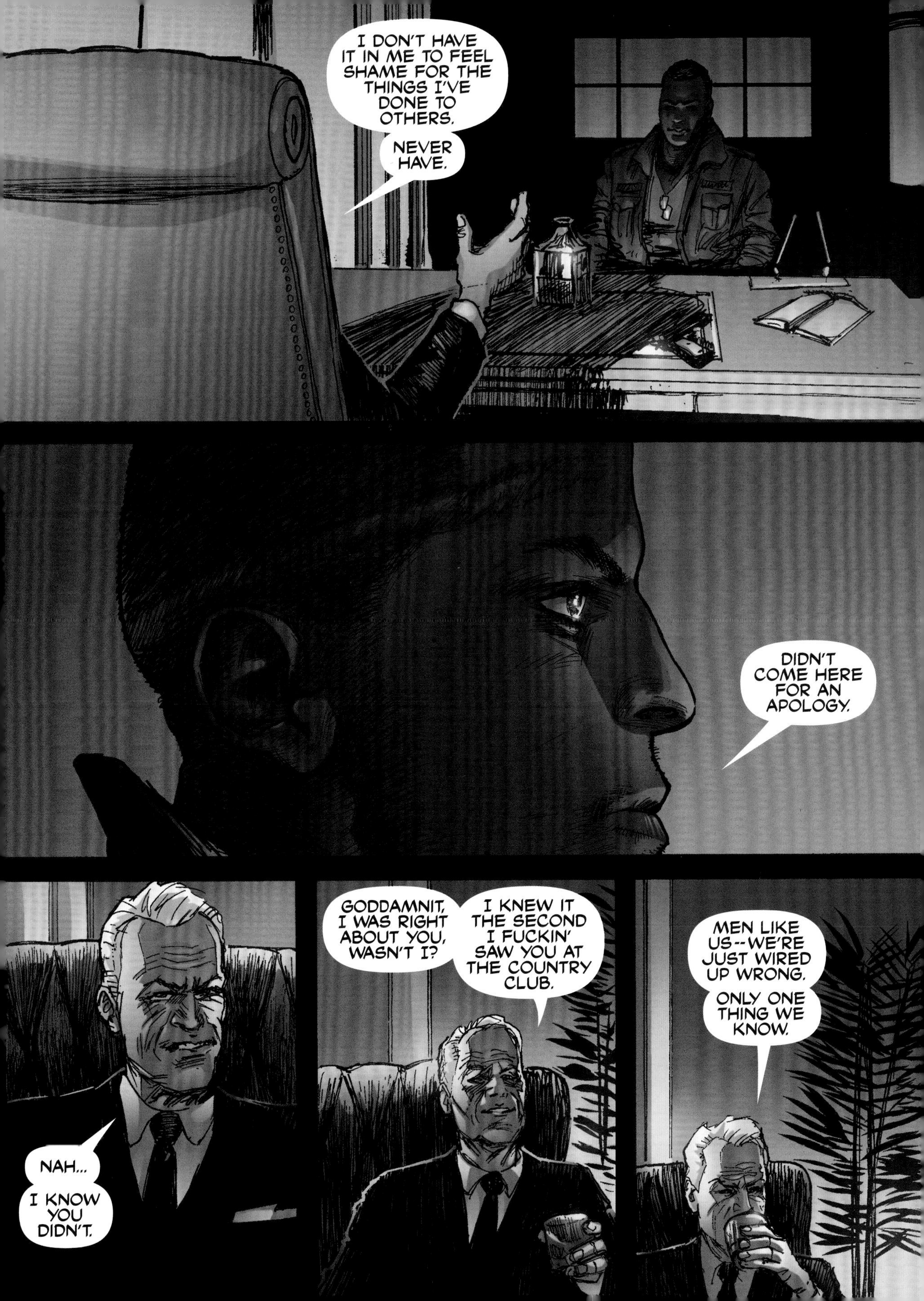
I DON'T HAVE IT IN ME TO FEEL SHAME FOR THE THINGS I'VE DONE TO OTHERS.
NEVER HAVE.
DIDN'T COME HERE FOR AN APOLOGY.
NAH...
I KNOW YOU DIDN'T.
GODDAMNIT, I WAS RIGHT ABOUT YOU, WASN'T I?
I KNEW IT THE SECOND I FUCKIN' SAW YOU AT THE COUNTRY CLUB.
MEN LIKE US--WE'RE JUST WIRED UP WRONG.
ONLY ONE THING WE KNOW.

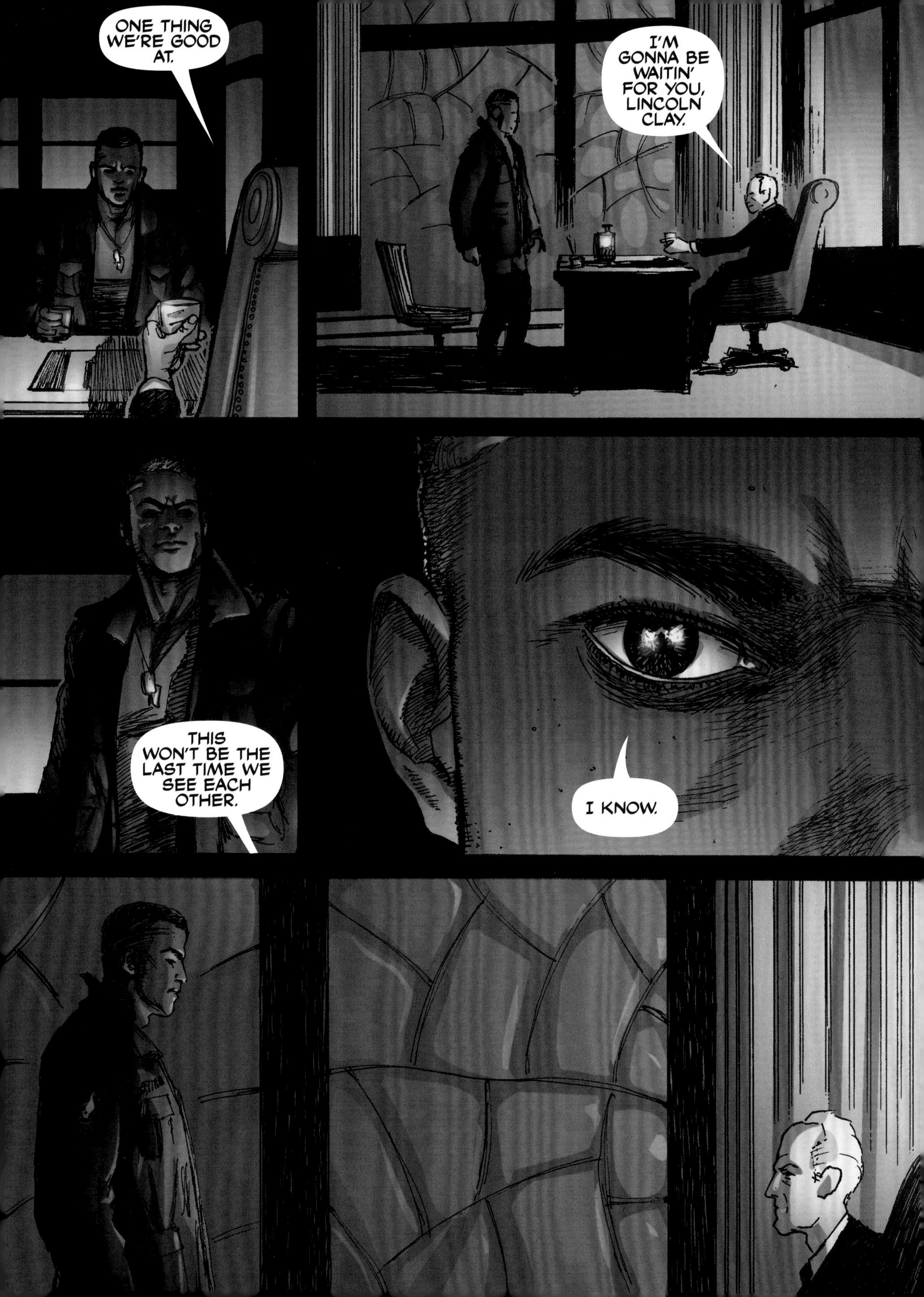
ONE THING WE'RE GOOD AT.
I'M GONNA BE WAITIN' FOR YOU, LINCOLN CLAY.
THIS WON'T BE THE LAST TIME WE SEE EACH OTHER.
I KNOW.

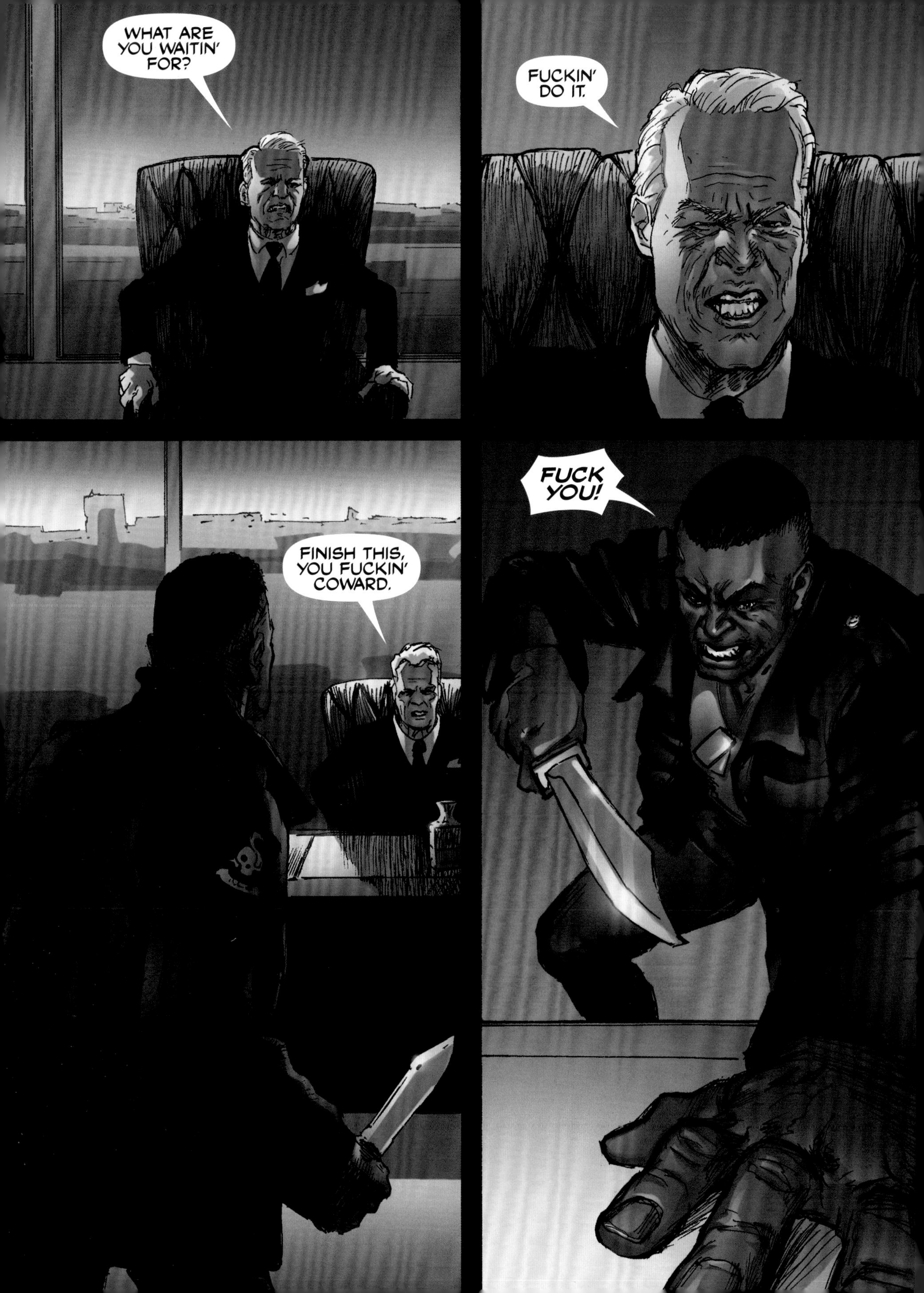
WHAT ARE YOU WAITIN' FOR?
FUCKIN' DO IT.
FINISH THIS, YOU FUCKIN' COWARD.
FUCK YOU!

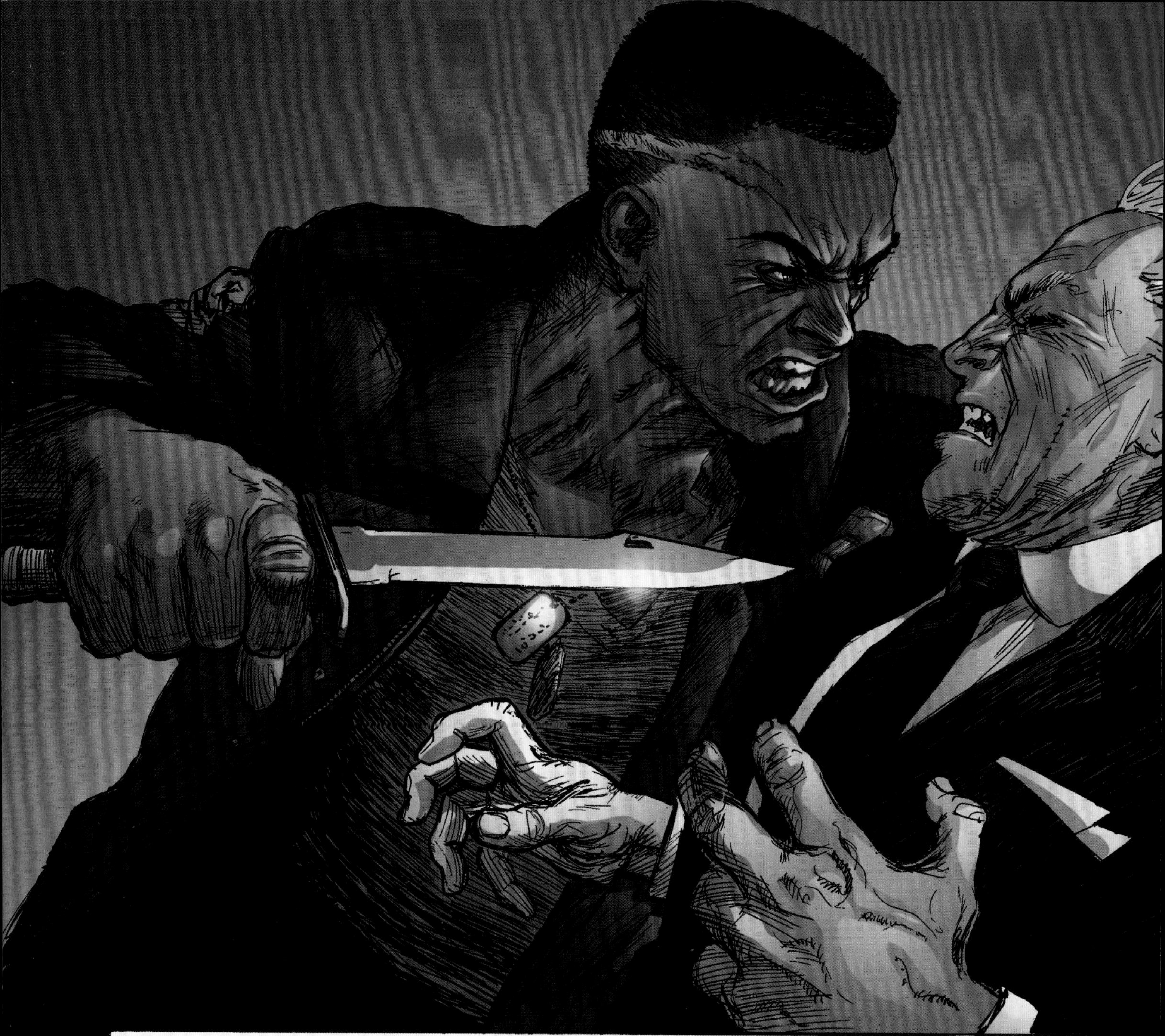

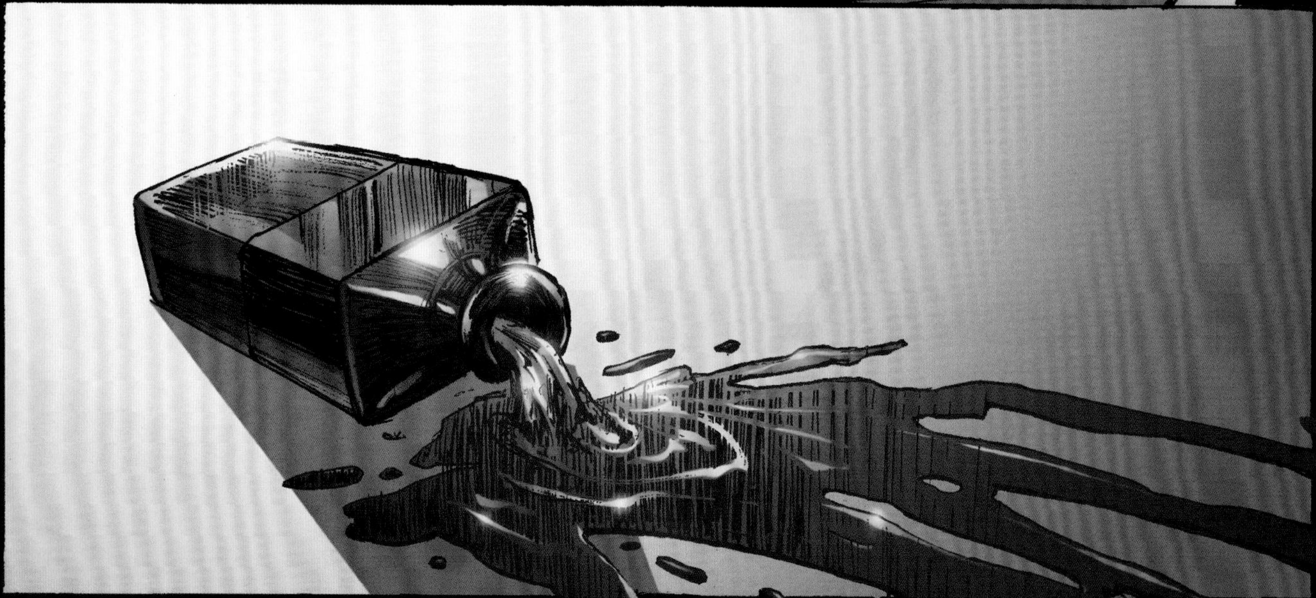

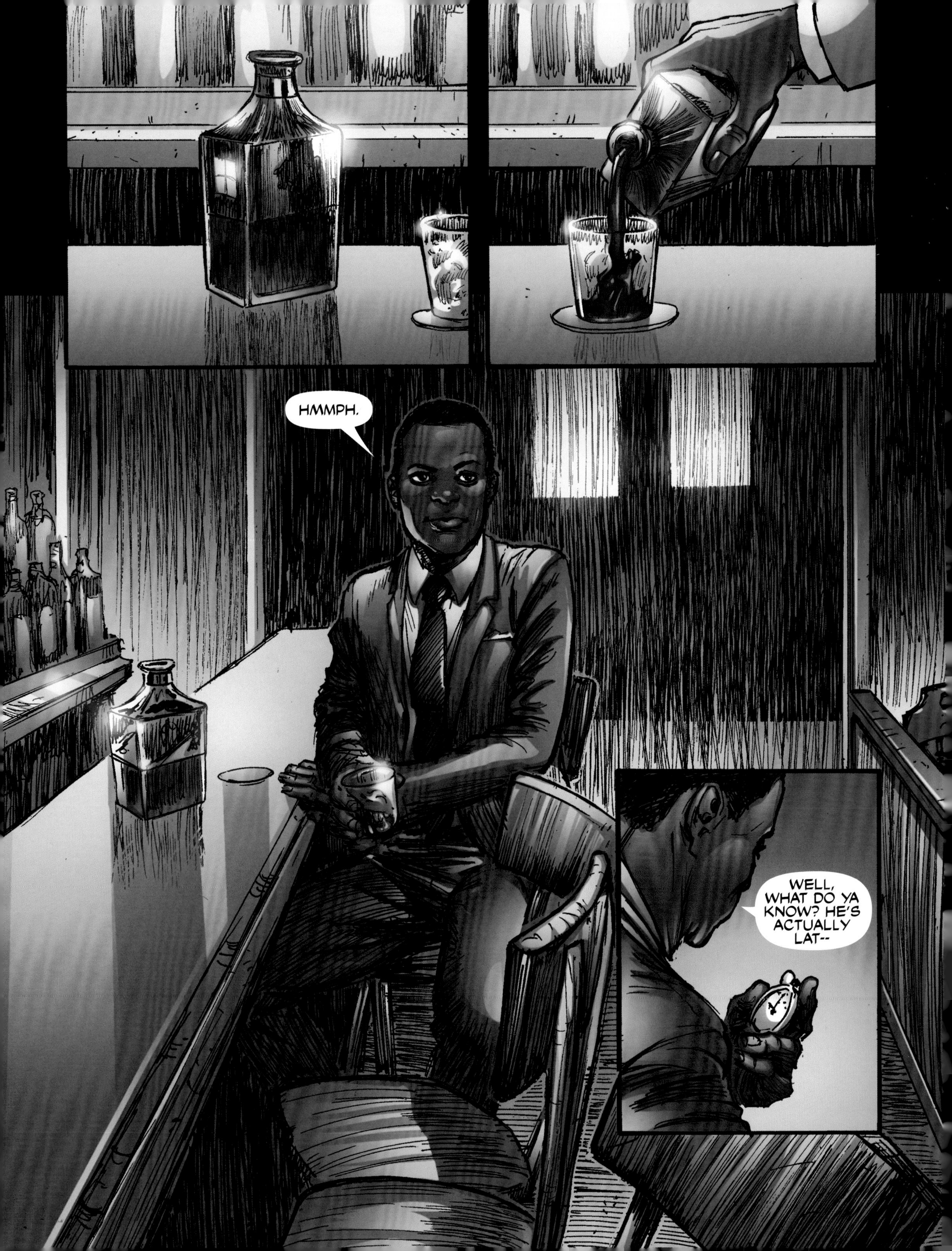
HMMPH.
WELL, WHAT DO YA KNOW? HE'S ACTUALLY LAT--

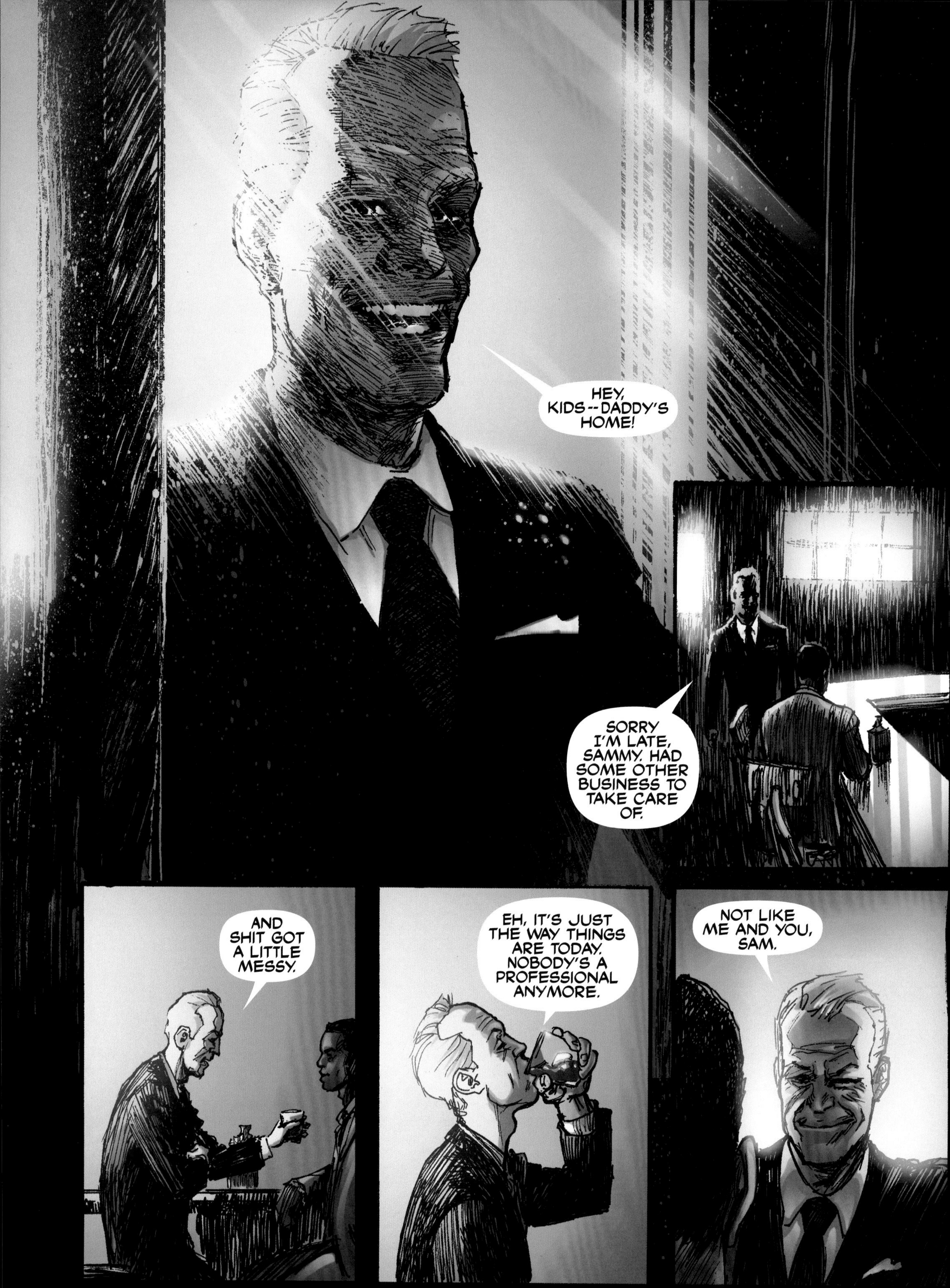
HEY, KIDS--DADDY'S HOME!
SORRY I'M LATE, SAMMY. HAD SOME OTHER BUSINESS TO TAKE CARE OF.
AND SHIT GOT A LITTLE MESSY.
EH, IT'S JUST THE WAY THINGS ARE TODAY. NOBODY'S A PROFESSIONAL ANYMORE.
NOT LIKE ME AND YOU, SAM.

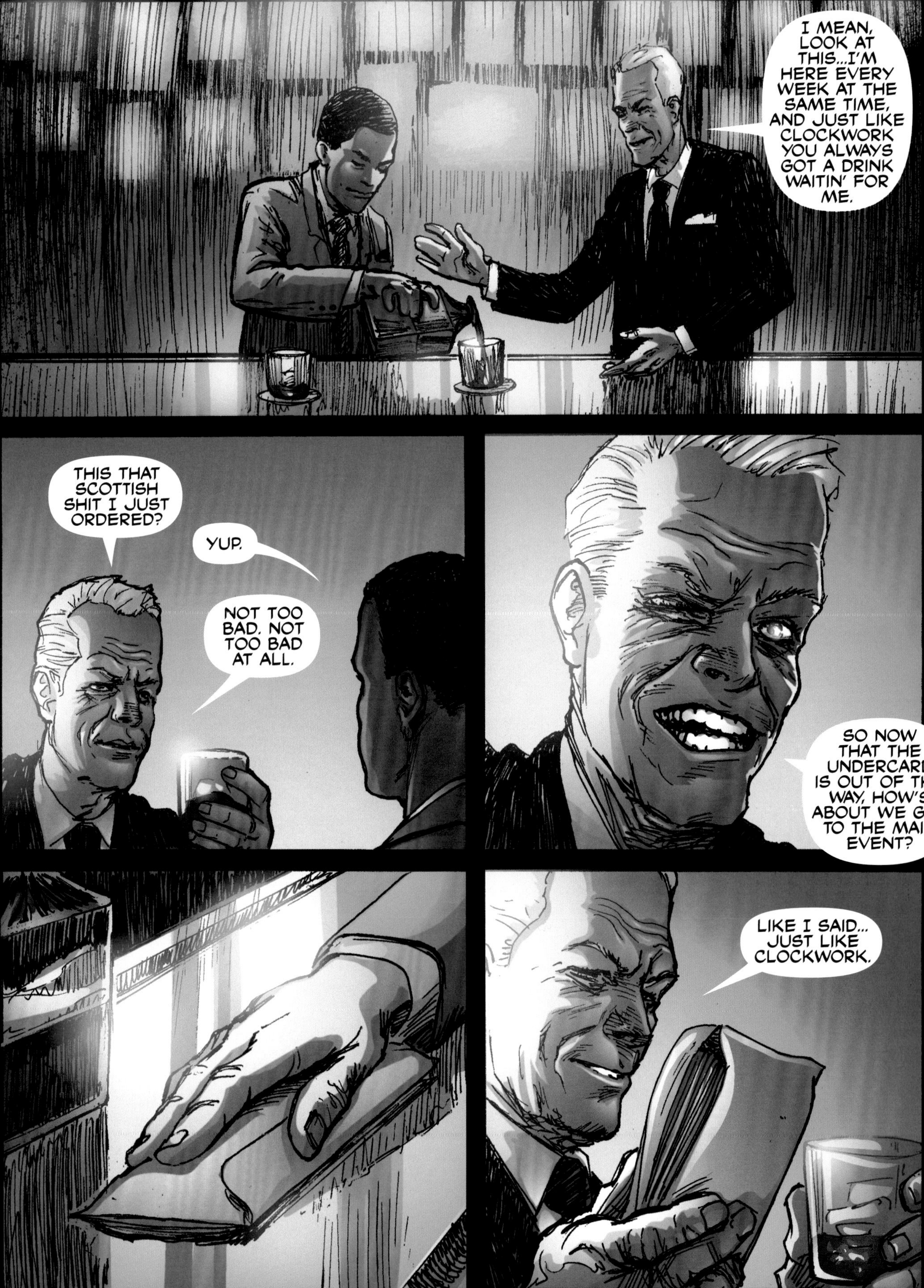
I MEAN, LOOK AT THIS...I'M HERE EVERY WEEK AT THE SAME TIME, AND JUST LIKE CLOCKWORK YOU ALWAYS GOT A DRINK WAITIN' FOR ME.
THIS THAT SCOTTISH SHIT I JUST ORDERED?
YUP.
NOT TOO BAD. NOT TOO BAD AT ALL.
SO NOW THAT THE UNDERCARD IS OUT OF THE WAY, HOW'S ABOUT WE GET TO THE MAIN EVENT?
LIKE I SAID... JUST LIKE CLOCKWORK.

LOTTERY LOOKS LIKE IT DONE PRETTY DAMN GOOD THIS WEEK. THEM HAITIAN COCKSUCKERS AIN'T STILL GIVIN' YA TROUBLE, ARE THEY?

CAN'T SAY I GOT ANY TROUBLE THESE DAYS, SAL.

WELL, AT LEAST THAT'S ONE OF US.

"US" HAS BEEN A LONG TIME, HUH, SAL? HOW LONG YOU FIGURE?

SHIT. I CAN'T REMEMBER. YOU'VE BEEN HERE SO FUCKIN' LONG I USED TO THINK THEY BUILT DELRAY HOLLOW AROUND THIS PLACE.

HEH. YOU'RE ONE TO TALK. I REMEMBER THE STORIES WHEN THE MARCANO BROTHERS HIT TOWN.

"ROARIN' TWENTIES," RIGHT?

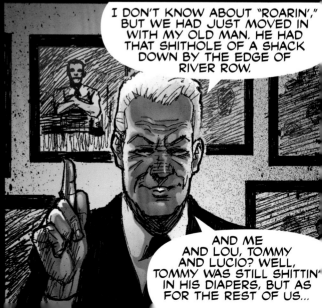

I DON'T KNOW ABOUT "ROARIN'," BUT WE HAD JUST MOVED IN WITH MY OLD MAN. HE HAD THAT SHITHOLE OF A SHACK DOWN BY THE EDGE OF RIVER ROW.

AND ME AND LOU, TOMMY AND LUCIO? WELL, TOMMY WAS STILL SHITTIN' IN HIS DIAPERS, BUT AS FOR THE REST OF US...

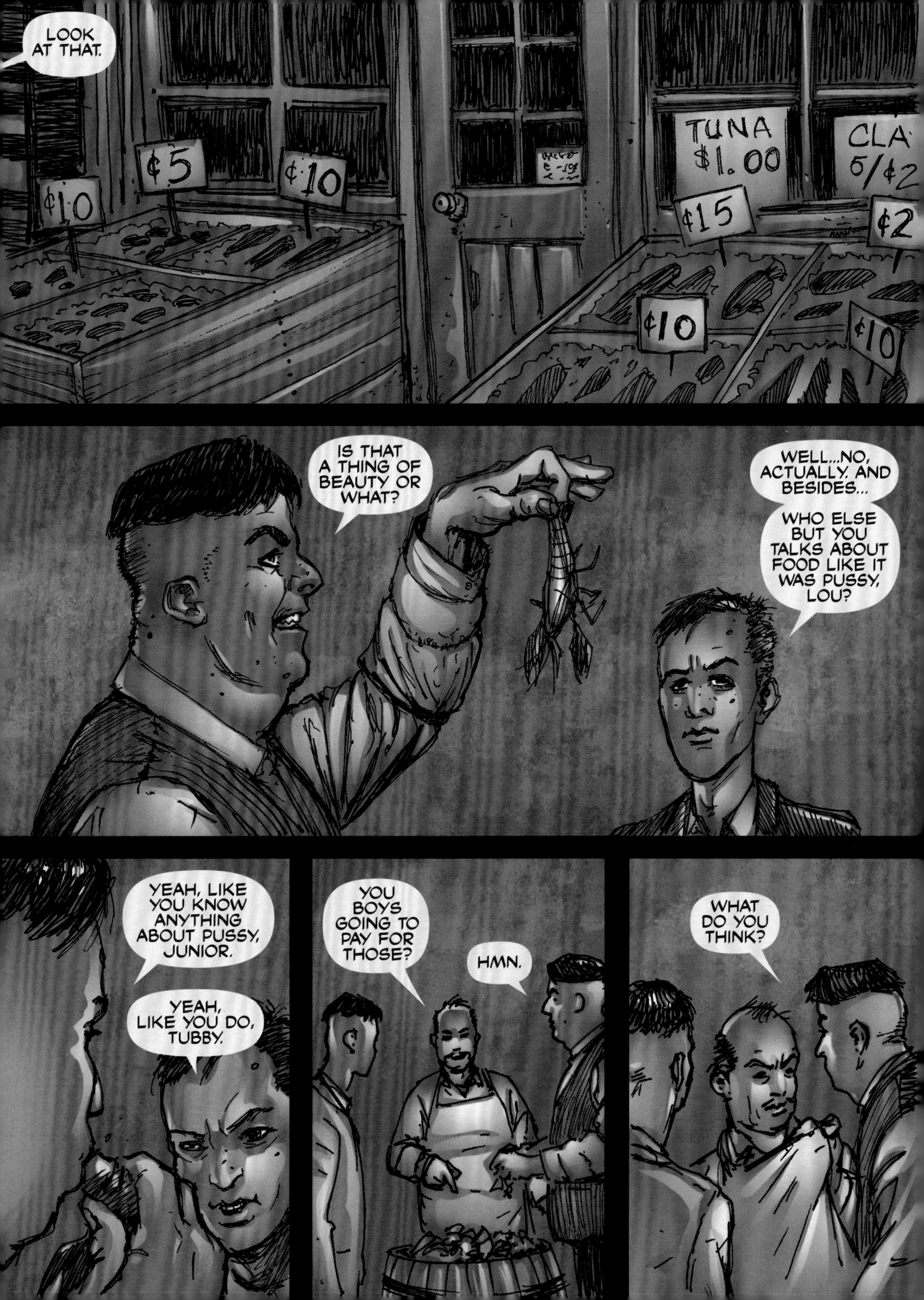

LOOK AT THAT.
¢10
¢5
¢10
TUNA $1.00
CLA 5/¢2
¢15
¢2
¢10
¢10
IS THAT A THING OF BEAUTY OR WHAT?
WELL...NO, ACTUALLY. AND BESIDES...
WHO ELSE BUT YOU TALKS ABOUT FOOD LIKE IT WAS PUSSY, LOU?
YEAH, LIKE YOU KNOW ANYTHING ABOUT PUSSY, JUNIOR.
YEAH, LIKE YOU DO, TUBBY.
YOU BOYS GOING TO PAY FOR THOSE?
HMN.
WHAT DO YOU THINK?

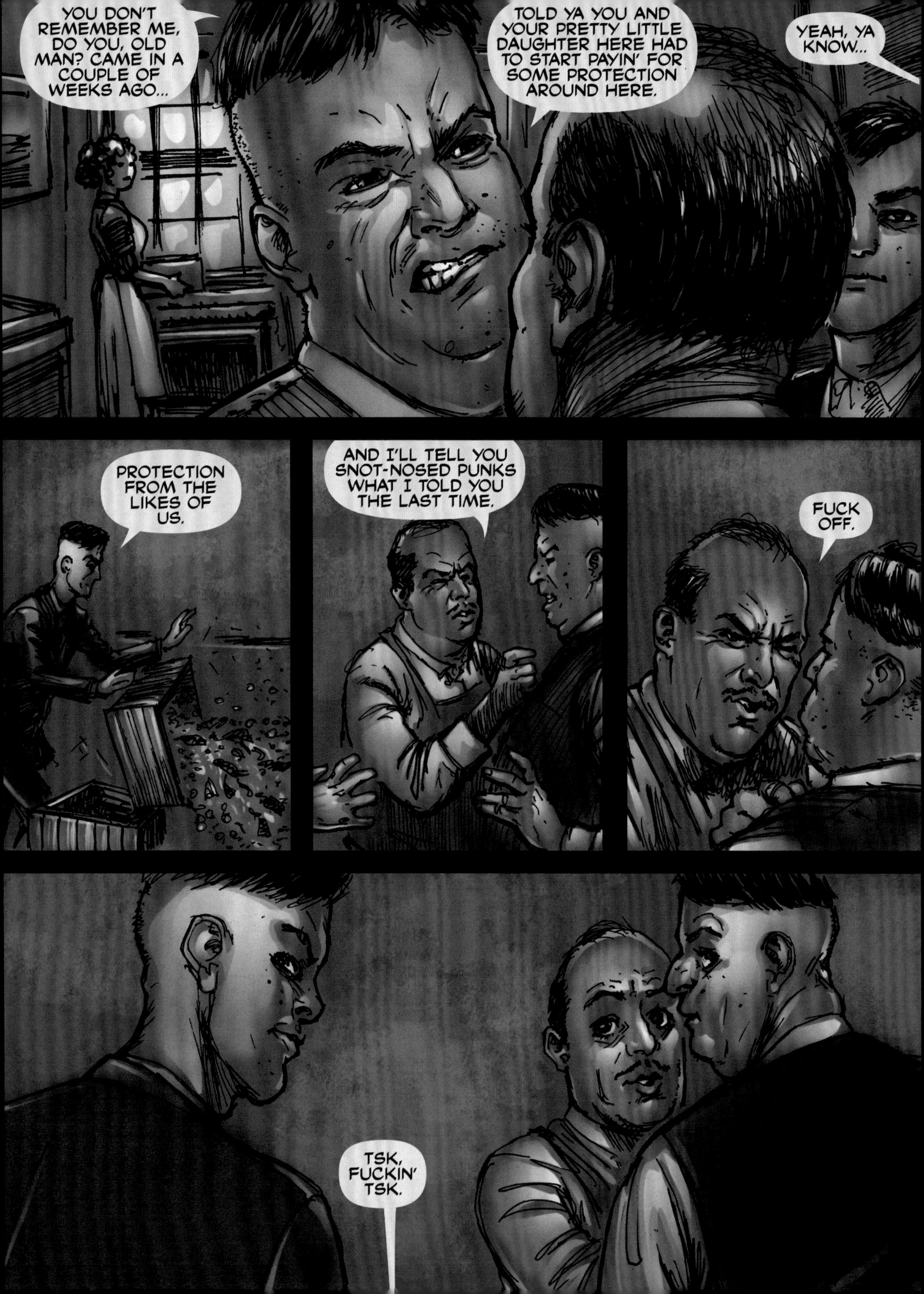
YOU DON'T REMEMBER ME, DO YOU, OLD MAN? CAME IN A COUPLE OF WEEKS AGO...
TOLD YA YOU AND YOUR PRETTY LITTLE DAUGHTER HERE HAD TO START PAYIN' FOR SOME PROTECTION AROUND HERE.
YEAH, YA KNOW...
PROTECTION FROM THE LIKES OF US.
AND I'LL TELL YOU SNOT-NOSED PUNKS WHAT I TOLD YOU THE LAST TIME.
FUCK OFF.
TSK, FUCKIN' TSK.

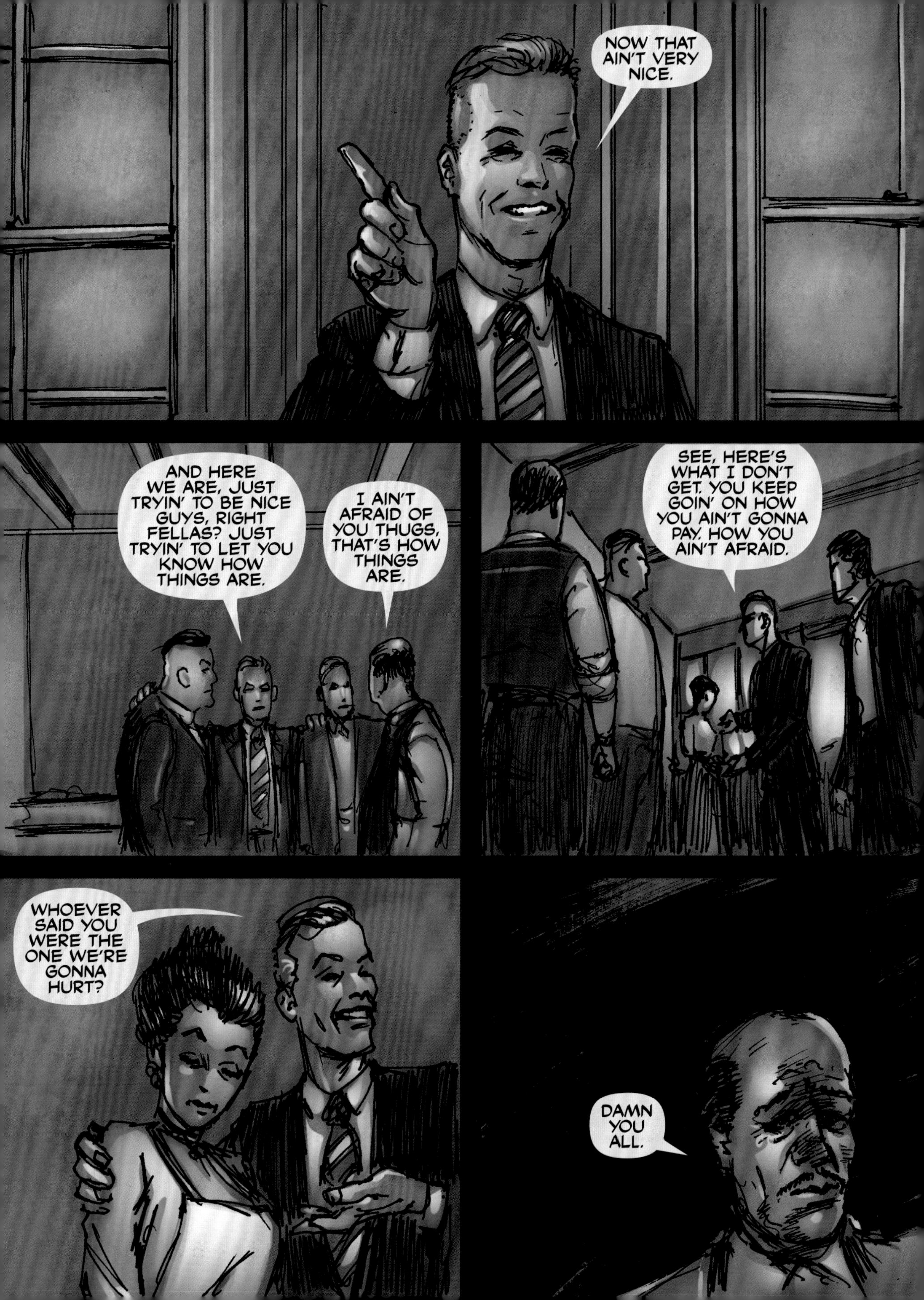
NOW THAT AIN'T VERY NICE.
AND HERE WE ARE, JUST TRYIN' TO BE NICE GUYS, RIGHT FELLAS? JUST TRYIN' TO LET YOU KNOW HOW THINGS ARE.
I AIN'T AFRAID OF YOU THUGS, THAT'S HOW THINGS ARE.
SEE, HERE'S WHAT I DON'T GET. YOU KEEP GOIN' ON HOW YOU AIN'T GONNA PAY. HOW YOU AIN'T AFRAID.
WHOEVER SAID YOU WERE THE ONE WE'RE GONNA HURT?
DAMN YOU ALL.

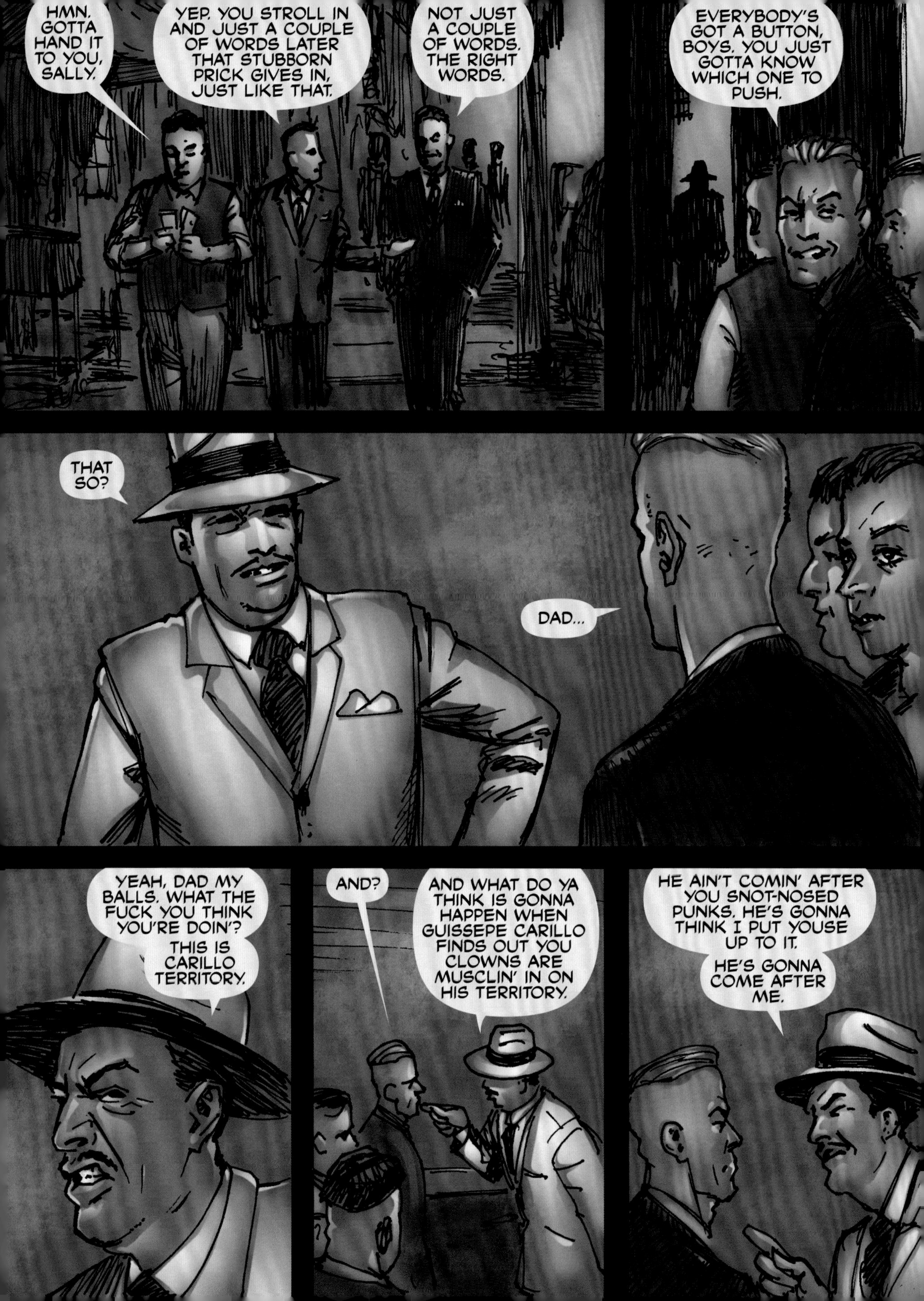
HMN, GOTTA HAND IT TO YOU, SALLY.
YEP. YOU STROLL IN AND JUST A COUPLE OF WORDS LATER THAT STUBBORN PRICK GIVES IN, JUST LIKE THAT.
NOT JUST A COUPLE OF WORDS. THE RIGHT WORDS.
EVERYBODY'S GOT A BUTTON, BOYS. YOU JUST GOTTA KNOW WHICH ONE TO PUSH.
THAT SO?
DAD...
YEAH, DAD MY BALLS. WHAT THE FUCK YOU THINK YOU'RE DOIN'?
THIS IS CARILLO TERRITORY.
AND?
AND WHAT DO YA THINK IS GONNA HAPPEN WHEN GUISSEPE CARILLO FINDS OUT YOU CLOWNS ARE MUSCLIN' IN ON HIS TERRITORY.
HE AIN'T COMIN' AFTER YOU SNOT-NOSED PUNKS. HE'S GONNA THINK I PUT YOUSE UP TO IT.
HE'S GONNA COME AFTER ME.

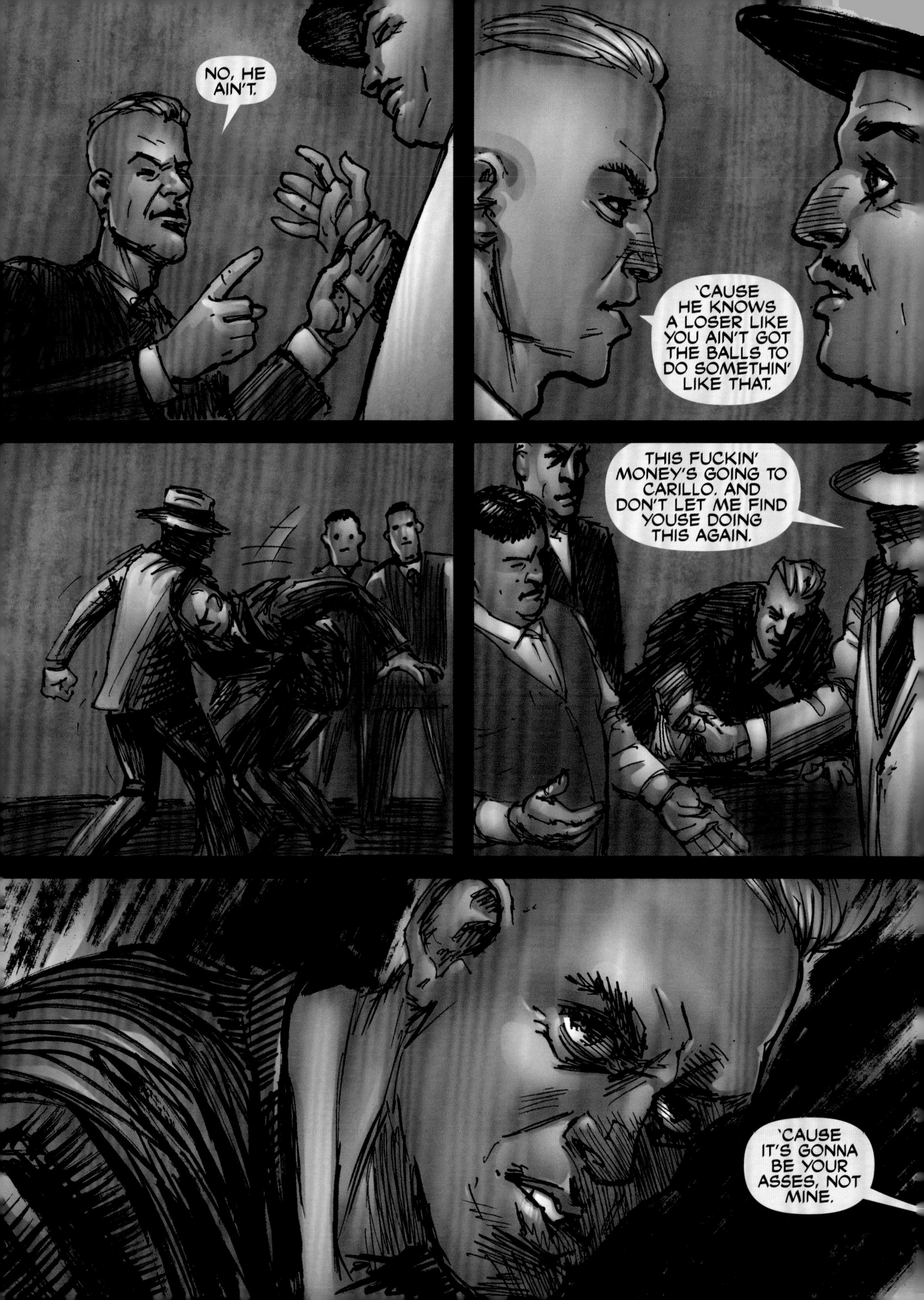
NO, HE AIN'T.
'CAUSE HE KNOWS A LOSER LIKE YOU AIN'T GOT THE BALLS TO DO SOMETHIN' LIKE THAT.
THIS FUCKIN' MONEY'S GOING TO CARILLO. AND DON'T LET ME FIND YOUSE DOING THIS AGAIN.
'CAUSE IT'S GONNA BE YOUR ASSES, NOT MINE.

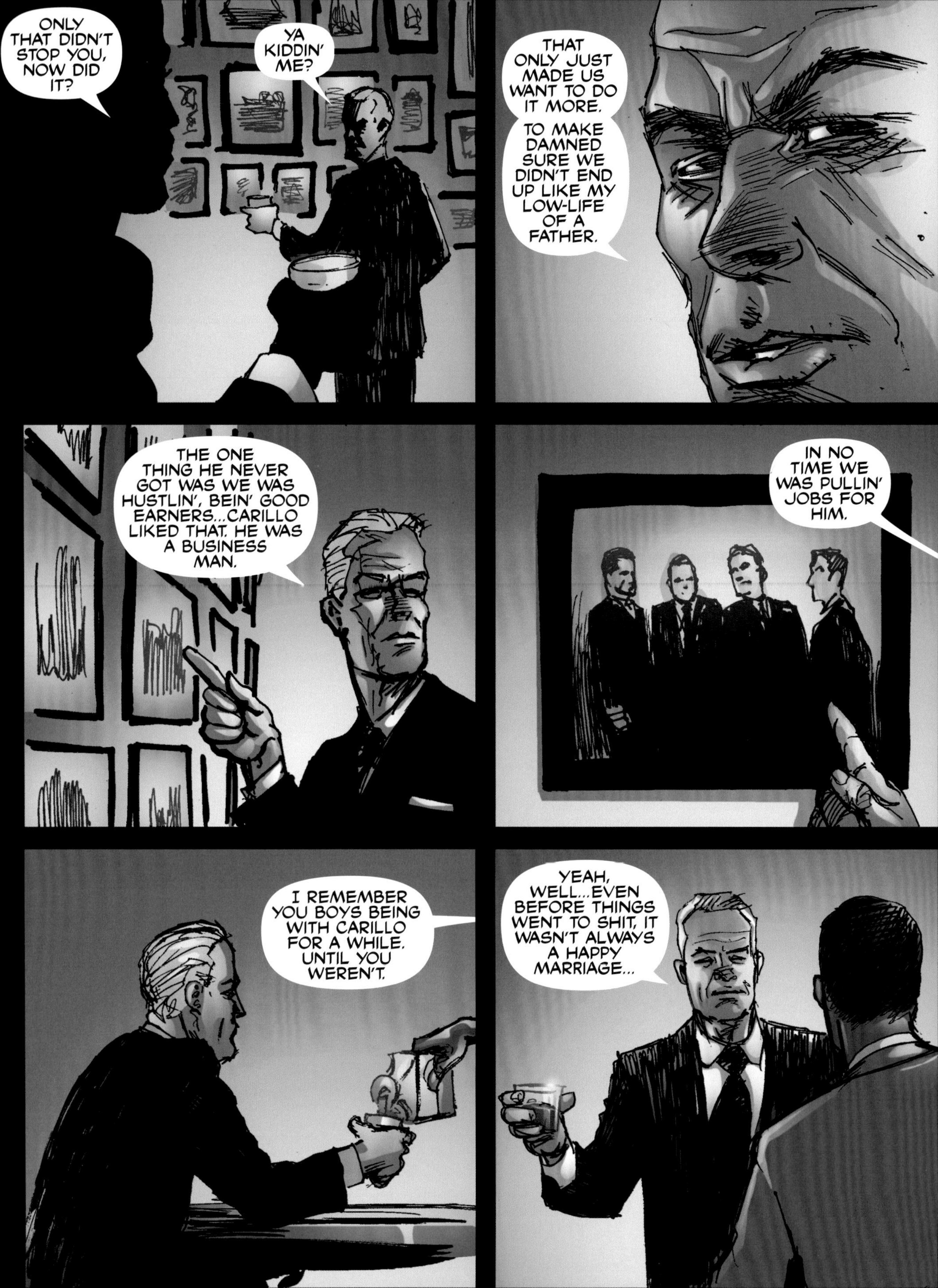
ONLY THAT DIDN'T STOP YOU, NOW DID IT?
YA KIDDIN' ME?
THAT ONLY JUST MADE US WANT TO DO IT MORE.
TO MAKE DAMNED SURE WE DIDN'T END UP LIKE MY LOW-LIFE OF A FATHER.
THE ONE THING HE NEVER GOT WAS WE WAS HUSTLIN', BEIN' GOOD EARNERS...CARILLO LIKED THAT. HE WAS A BUSINESS MAN.
IN NO TIME WE WAS PULLIN' JOBS FOR HIM.
I REMEMBER YOU BOYS BEING WITH CARILLO FOR A WHILE. UNTIL YOU WEREN'T.
YEAH, WELL...EVEN BEFORE THINGS WENT TO SHIT, IT WASN'T ALWAYS A HAPPY MARRIAGE...

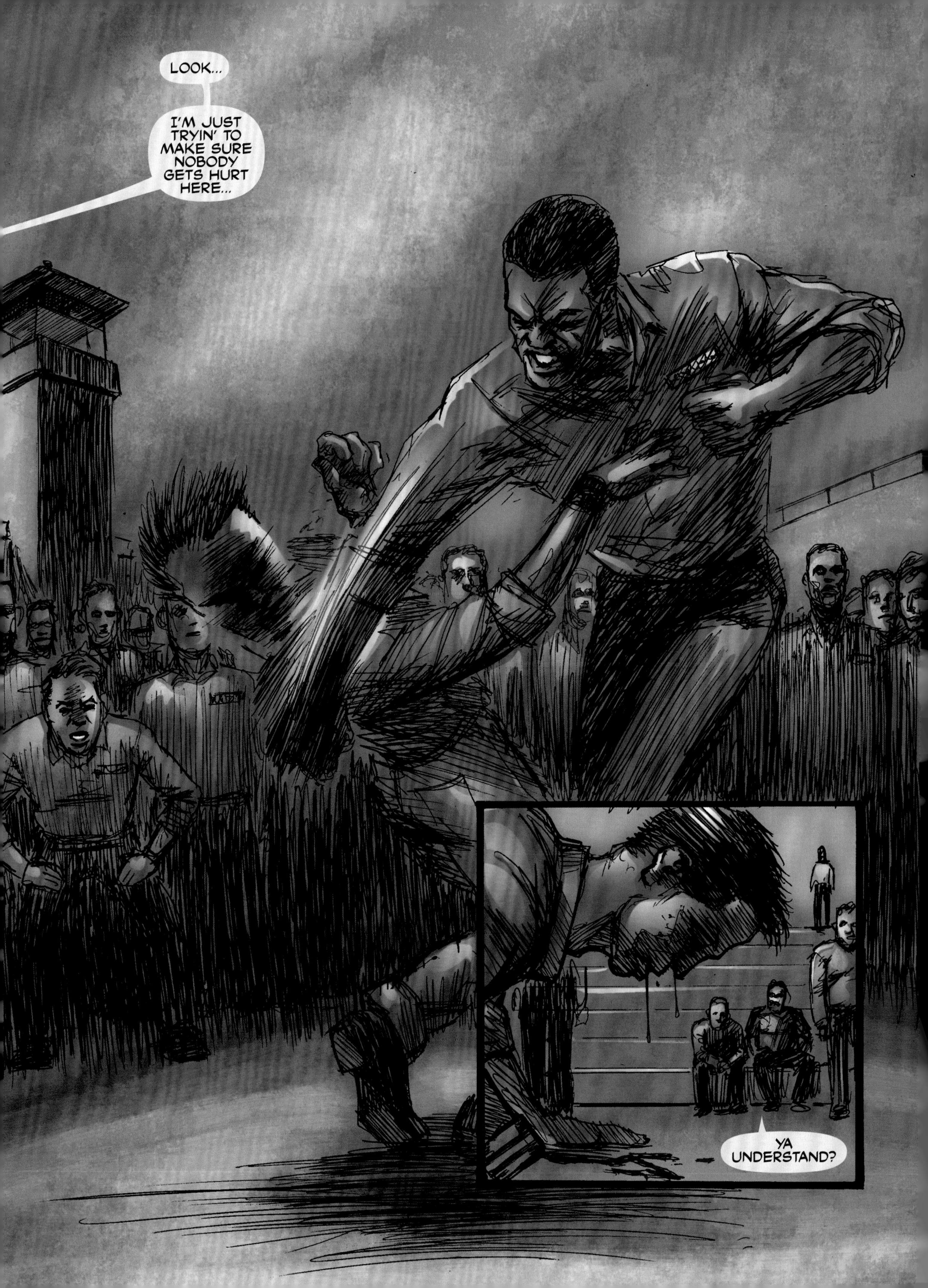
LOOK...
I'M JUST TRYIN' TO MAKE SURE NOBODY GETS HURT HERE...
YA UNDERSTAND?

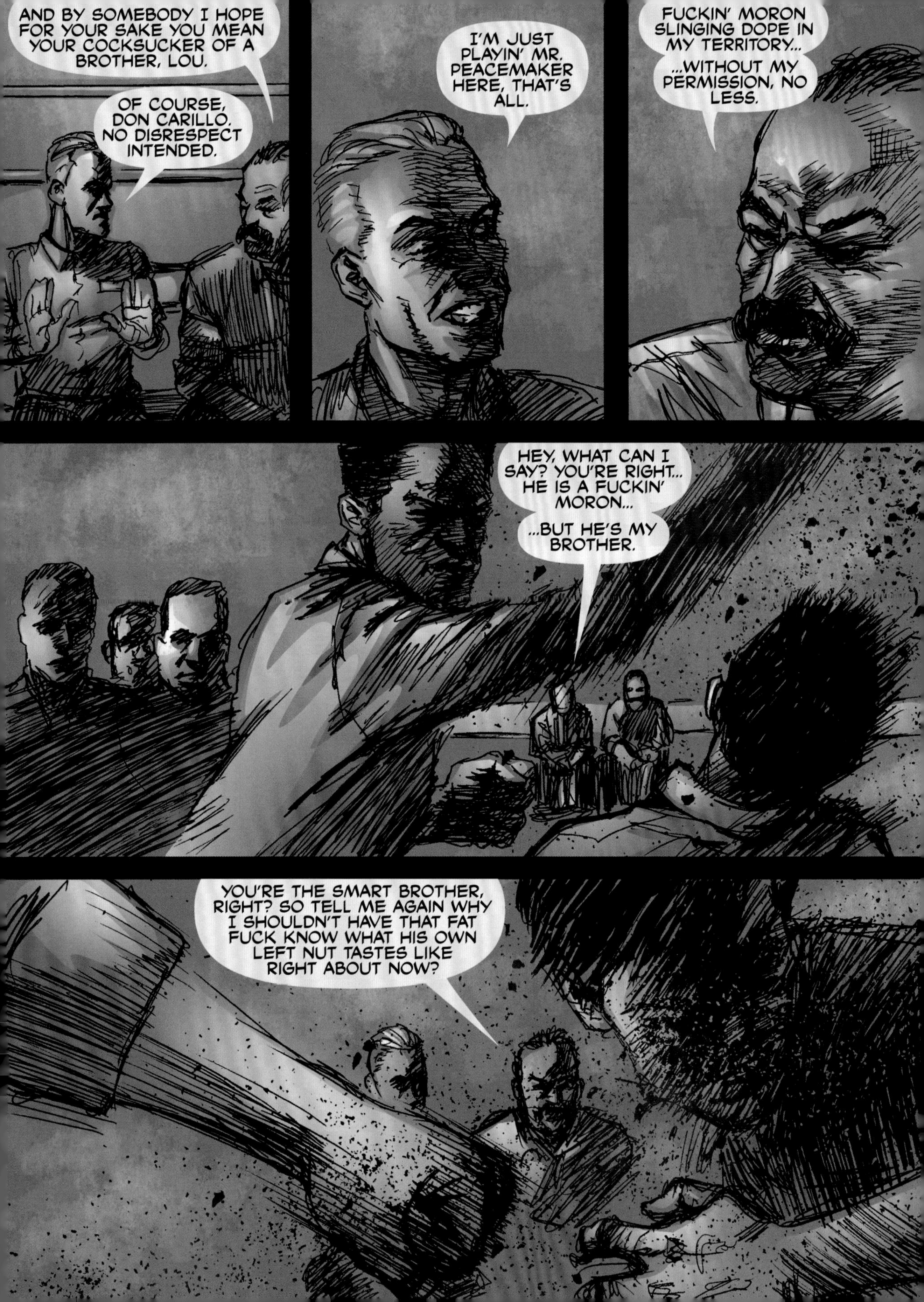
AND BY SOMEBODY I HOPE FOR YOUR SAKE YOU MEAN YOUR COCKSUCKER OF A BROTHER, LOU.
OF COURSE, DON CARILLO. NO DISRESPECT INTENDED.
I'M JUST PLAYIN' MR. PEACEMAKER HERE, THAT'S ALL.
FUCKIN' MORON SLINGING DOPE IN MY TERRITORY...
...WITHOUT MY PERMISSION, NO LESS.
HEY, WHAT CAN I SAY? YOU'RE RIGHT... HE IS A FUCKIN' MORON...
...BUT HE'S MY BROTHER.
YOU'RE THE SMART BROTHER, RIGHT? SO TELL ME AGAIN WHY I SHOULDN'T HAVE THAT FAT FUCK KNOW WHAT HIS OWN LEFT NUT TASTES LIKE RIGHT ABOUT NOW?

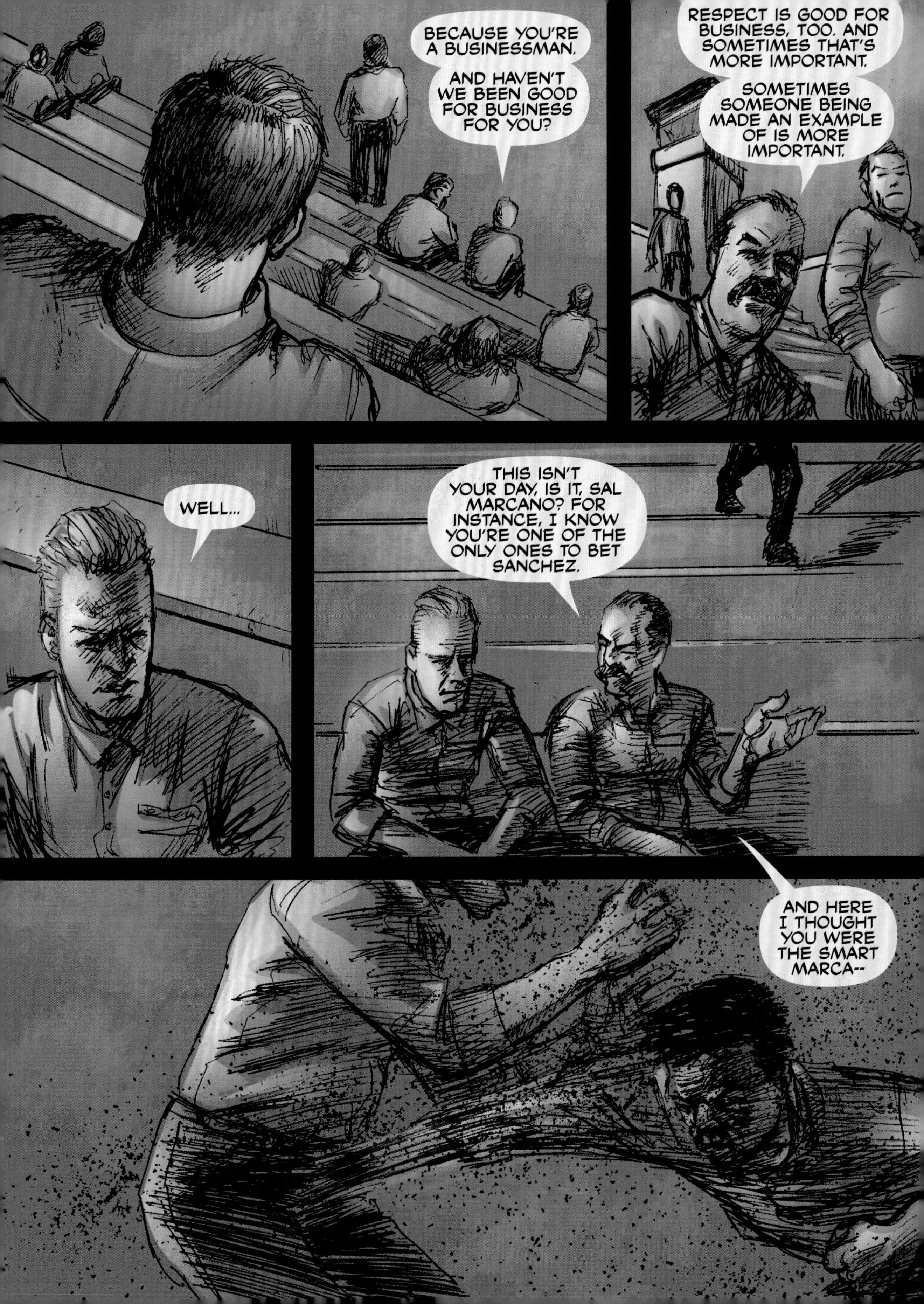
BECAUSE YOU'RE A BUSINESSMAN.
AND HAVEN'T WE BEEN GOOD FOR BUSINESS FOR YOU?
RESPECT IS GOOD FOR BUSINESS, TOO. AND SOMETIMES THAT'S MORE IMPORTANT.
SOMETIMES SOMEONE BEING MADE AN EXAMPLE OF IS MORE IMPORTANT.
WELL...
THIS ISN'T YOUR DAY, IS IT, SAL MARCANO? FOR INSTANCE, I KNOW YOU'RE ONE OF THE ONLY ONES TO BET SANCHEZ.
AND HERE I THOUGHT YOU WERE THE SMART MARCA--

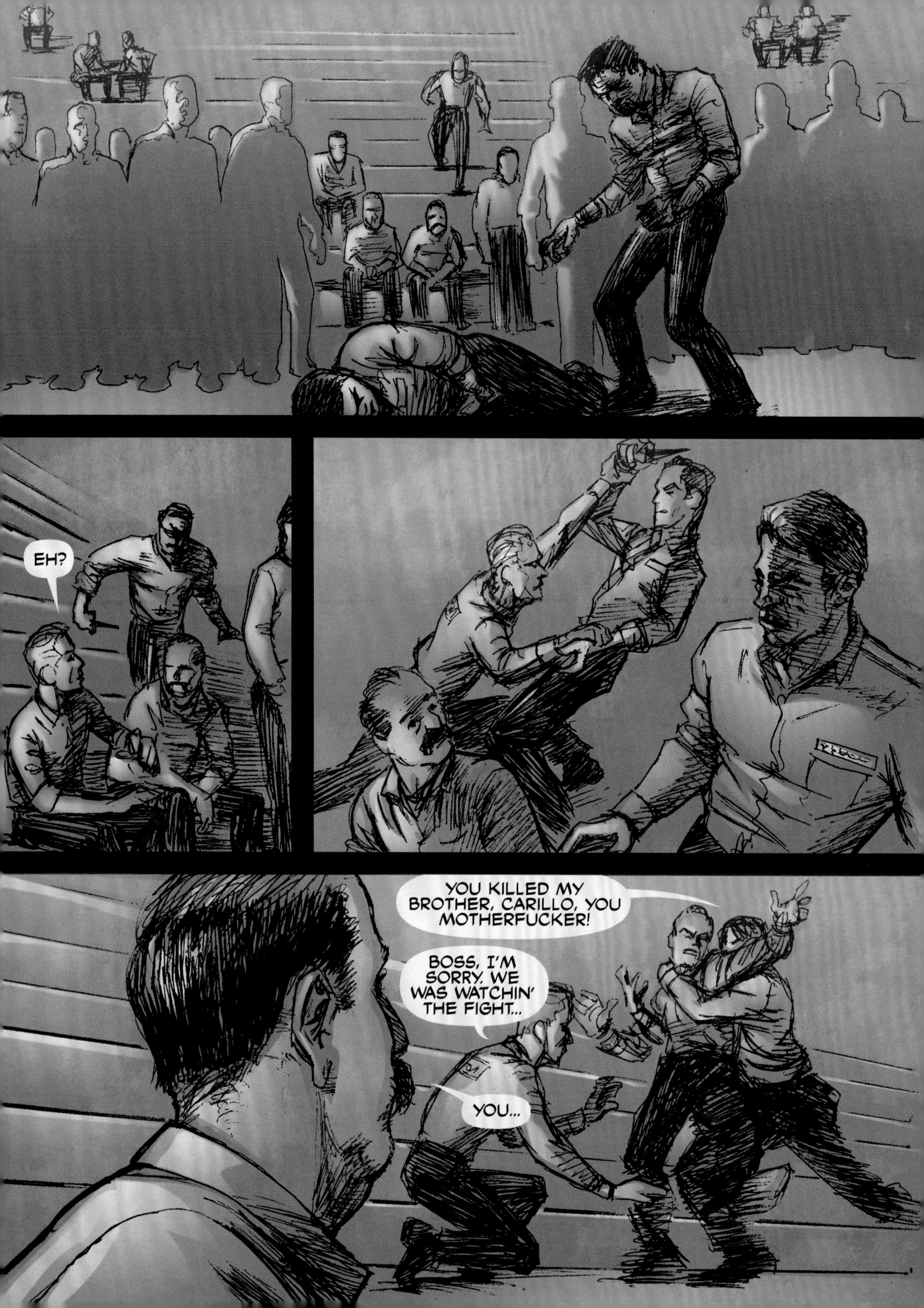
EH?
YOU KILLED MY BROTHER, CARILLO, YOU MOTHERFUCKER!
BOSS, I'M SORRY. WE WAS WATCHIN' THE FIGHT...
YOU...

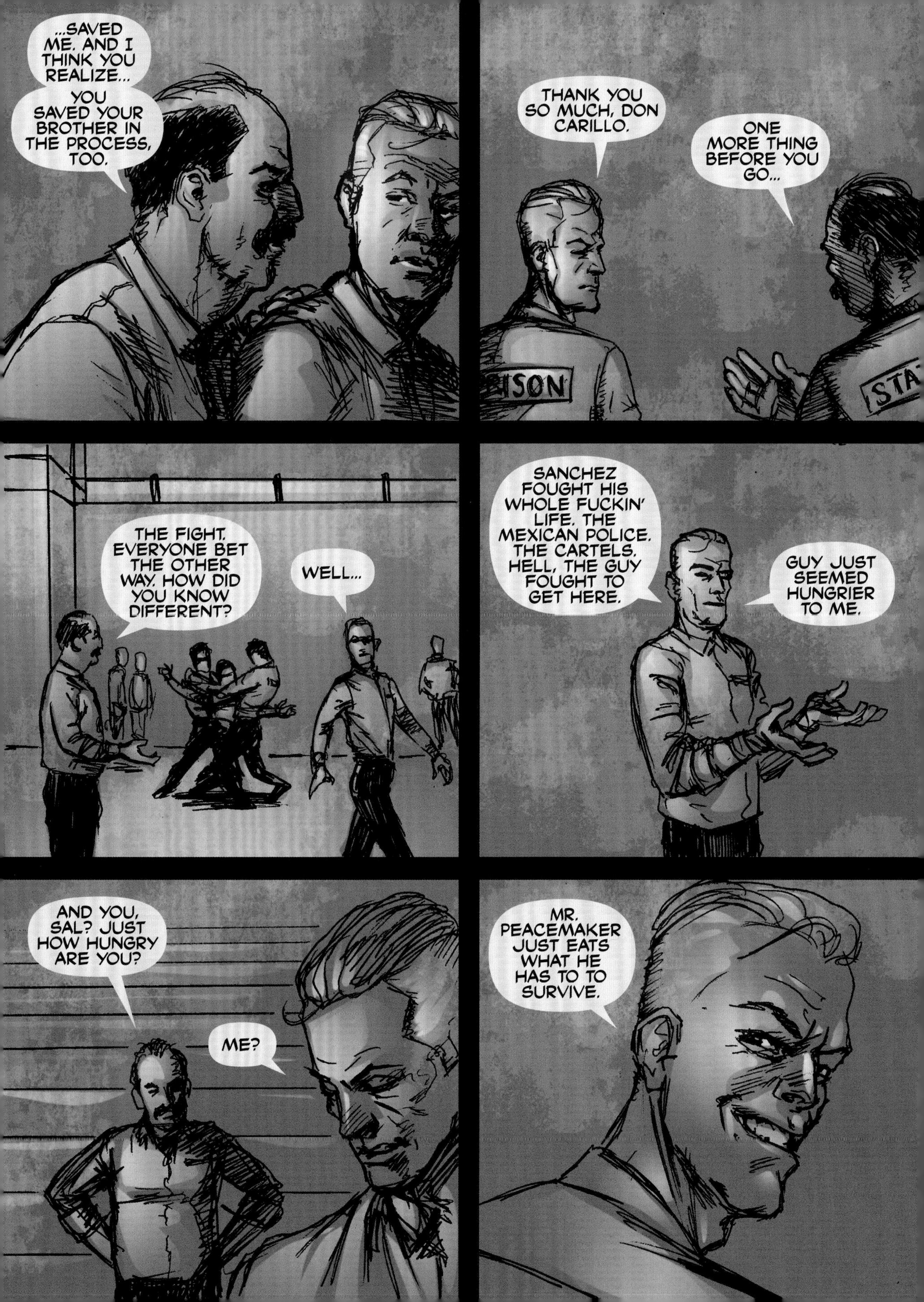

...SAVED ME. AND I THINK YOU REALIZE...
YOU SAVED YOUR BROTHER IN THE PROCESS, TOO.
THANK YOU SO MUCH, DON CARILLO.
ONE MORE THING BEFORE YOU GO...
NSON
STA
THE FIGHT. EVERYONE BET THE OTHER WAY. HOW DID YOU KNOW DIFFERENT?
WELL...
SANCHEZ FOUGHT HIS WHOLE FUCKIN' LIFE. THE MEXICAN POLICE. THE CARTELS. HELL, THE GUY FOUGHT TO GET HERE.
GUY JUST SEEMED HUNGRIER TO ME.
AND YOU, SAL? JUST HOW HUNGRY ARE YOU?
ME?
MR. PEACEMAKER JUST EATS WHAT HE HAS TO TO SURVIVE.

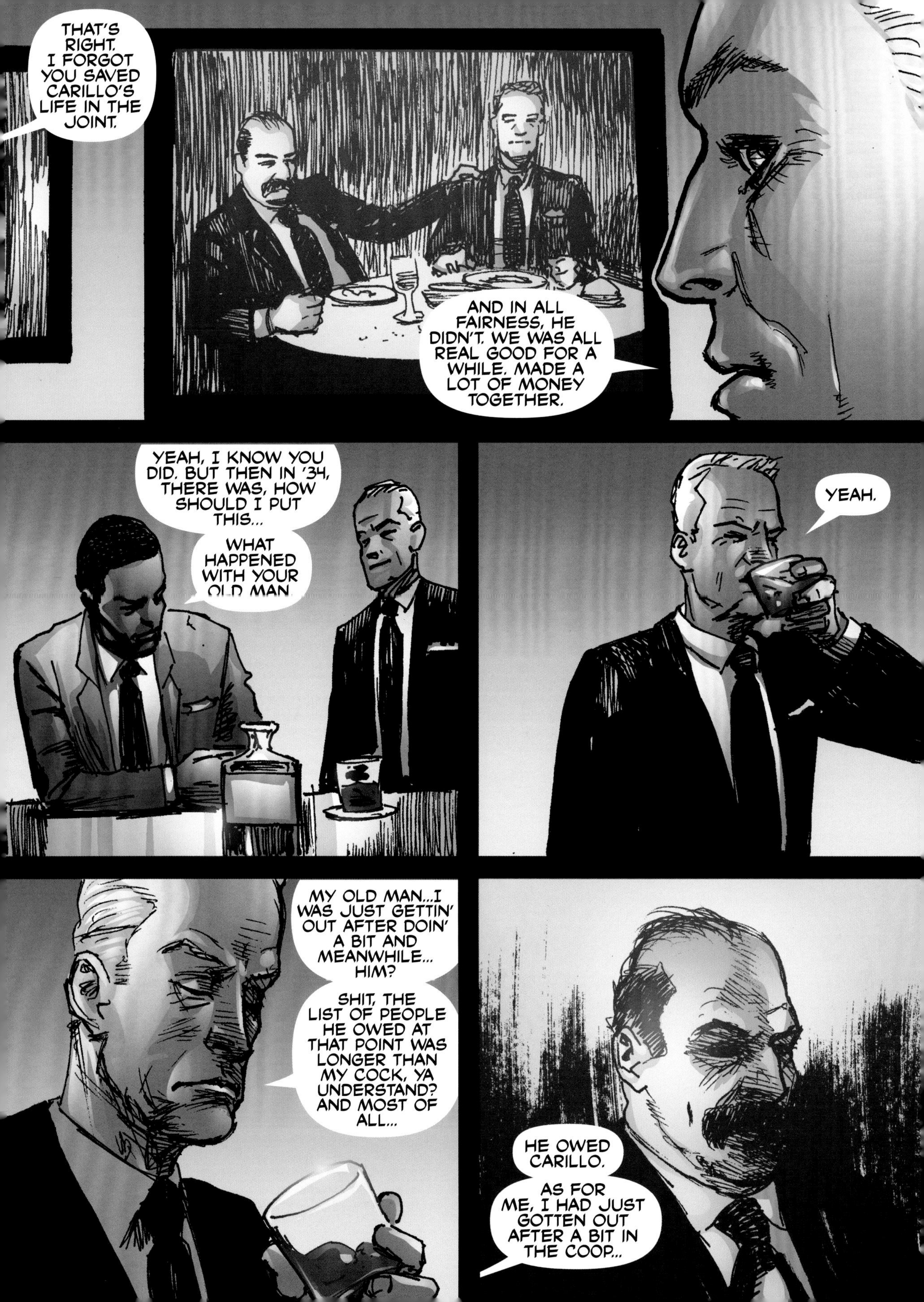
THAT'S RIGHT. I FORGOT YOU SAVED CARILLO'S LIFE IN THE JOINT.
AND IN ALL FAIRNESS, HE DIDN'T. WE WAS ALL REAL GOOD FOR A WHILE. MADE A LOT OF MONEY TOGETHER.
YEAH, I KNOW YOU DID. BUT THEN IN '34, THERE WAS, HOW SHOULD I PUT THIS...
WHAT HAPPENED WITH YOUR OLD MAN.
YEAH.
MY OLD MAN...I WAS JUST GETTIN' OUT AFTER DOIN' A BIT AND MEANWHILE... HIM?
SHIT, THE LIST OF PEOPLE HE OWED AT THAT POINT WAS LONGER THAN MY COCK, YA UNDERSTAND? AND MOST OF ALL...
HE OWED CARILLO.
AS FOR ME, I HAD JUST GOTTEN OUT AFTER A BIT IN THE COOP...

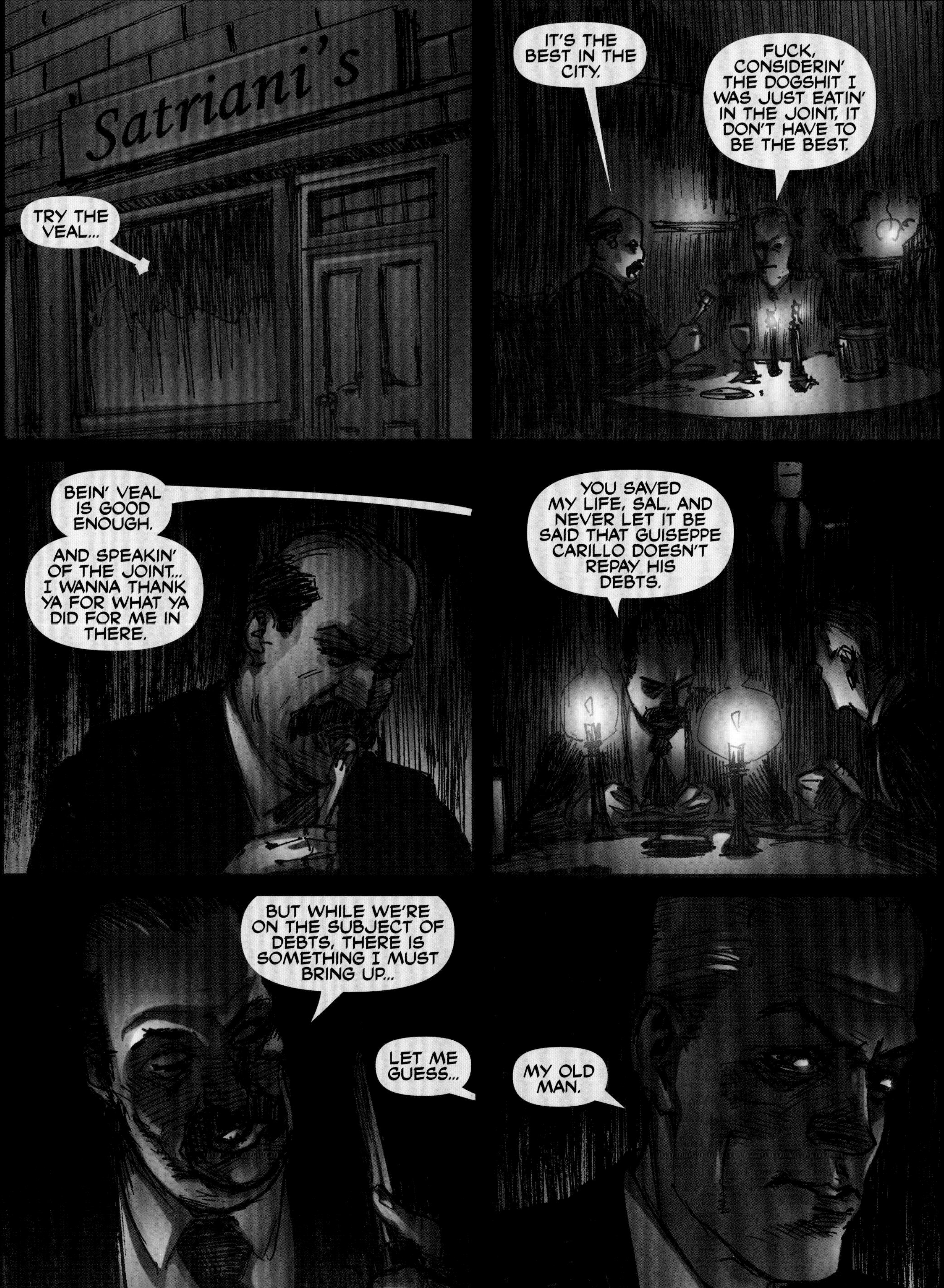
Satriani's
TRY THE VEAL...
IT'S THE BEST IN THE CITY.
FUCK, CONSIDERIN' THE DOGSHIT I WAS JUST EATIN' IN THE JOINT, IT DON'T HAVE TO BE THE BEST.
BEIN' VEAL IS GOOD ENOUGH.
AND SPEAKIN' OF THE JOINT... I WANNA THANK YA FOR WHAT YA DID FOR ME IN THERE.
YOU SAVED MY LIFE, SAL. AND NEVER LET IT BE SAID THAT GUISEPPE CARILLO DOESN'T REPAY HIS DEBTS.
BUT WHILE WE'RE ON THE SUBJECT OF DEBTS, THERE IS SOMETHING I MUST BRING UP...
LET ME GUESS...
MY OLD MAN.

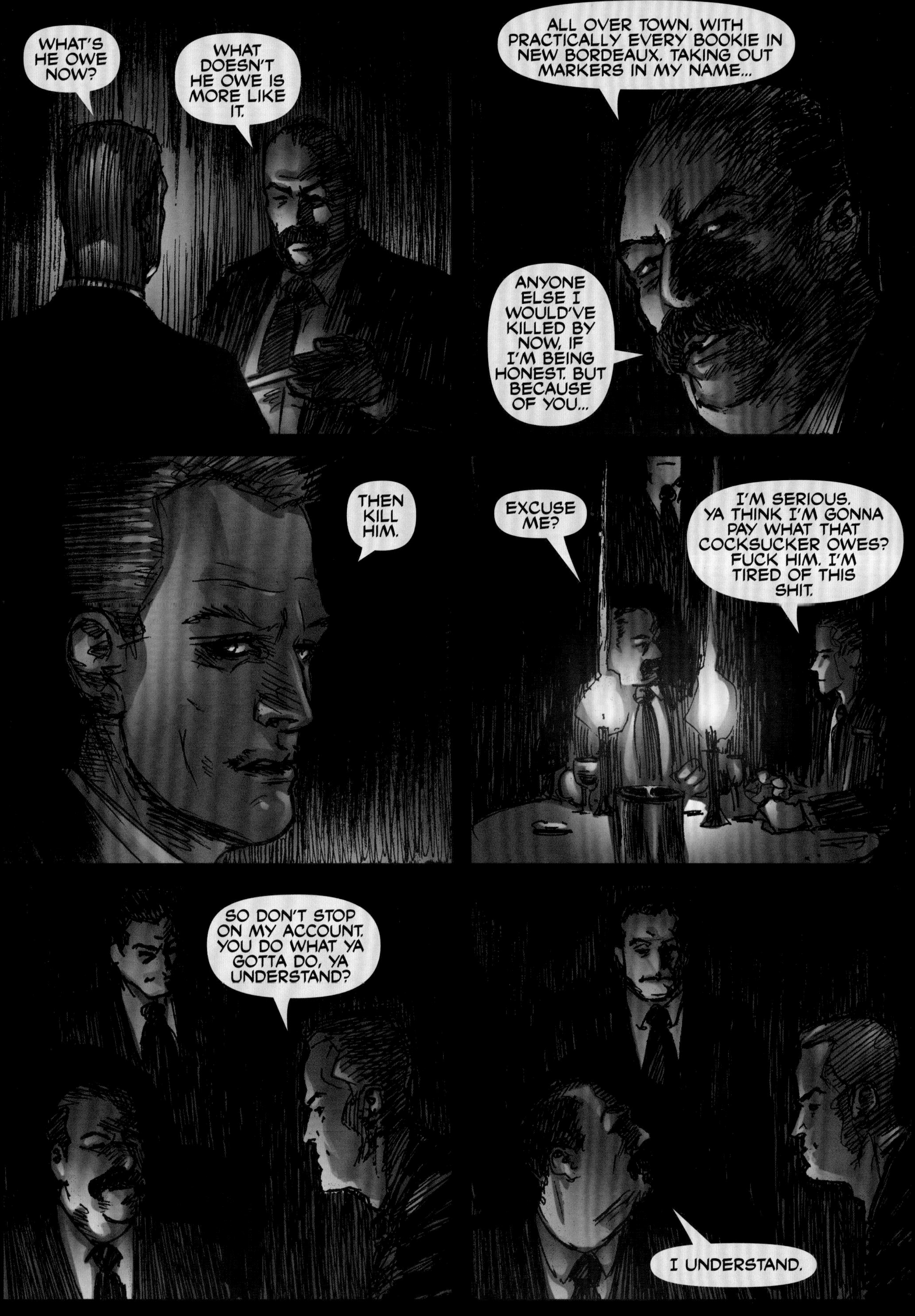
WHAT'S HE OWE NOW?
WHAT DOESN'T HE OWE IS MORE LIKE IT.
ALL OVER TOWN. WITH PRACTICALLY EVERY BOOKIE IN NEW BORDEAUX. TAKING OUT MARKERS IN MY NAME...
ANYONE ELSE I WOULD'VE KILLED BY NOW, IF I'M BEING HONEST. BUT BECAUSE OF YOU...
THEN KILL HIM.
EXCUSE ME?
I'M SERIOUS. YA THINK I'M GONNA PAY WHAT THAT COCKSUCKER OWES? FUCK HIM. I'M TIRED OF THIS SHIT.
SO DON'T STOP ON MY ACCOUNT. YOU DO WHAT YA GOTTA DO, YA UNDERSTAND?
I UNDERSTAND.

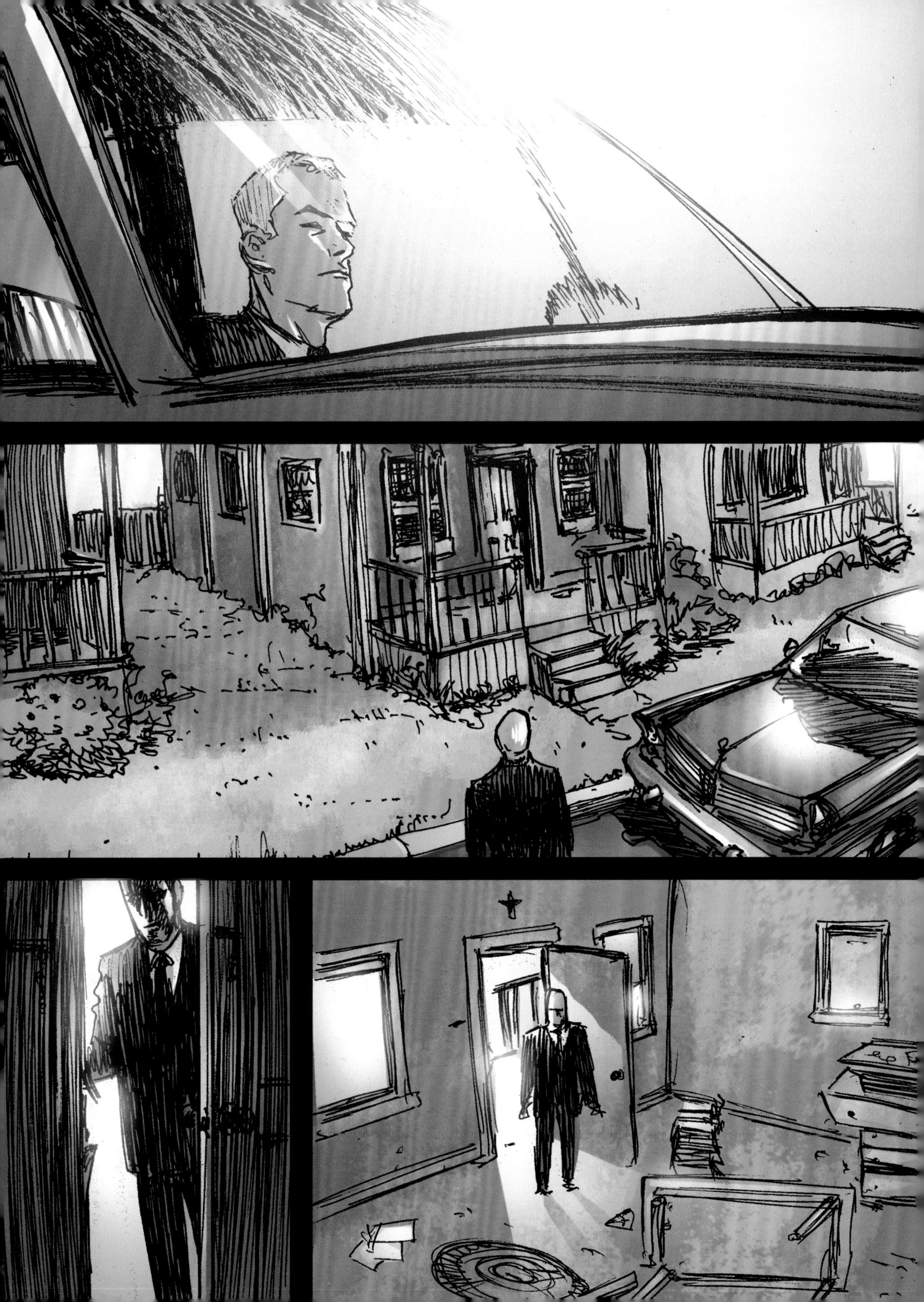

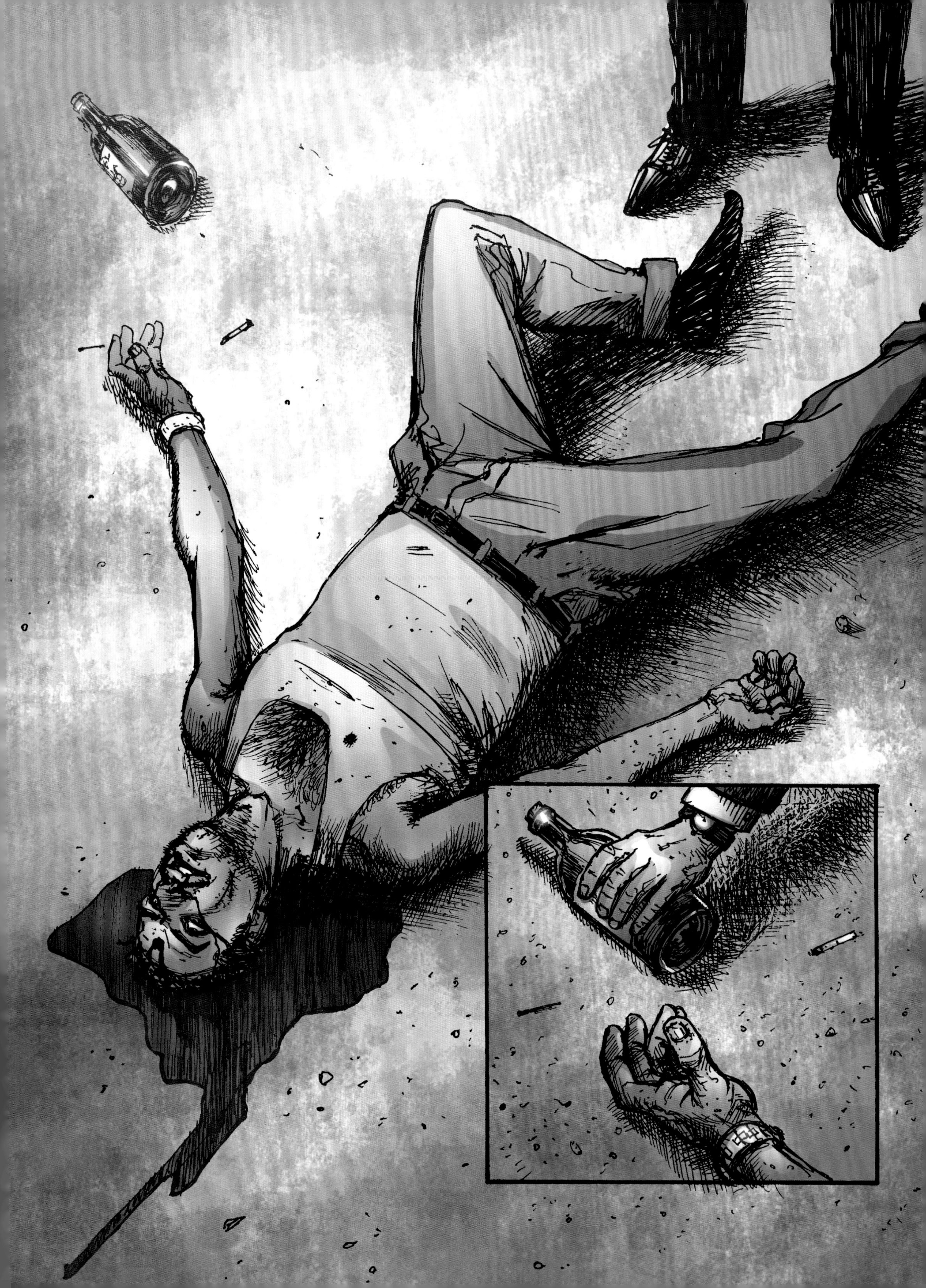

LOU?
LOU,
JESUS
CHRIST,
LOU...

IT'S
DAD.

FUCKIN'
CARILLO, MAN.
I PLEADED
WITH HIM NOT
TO WHACK
HIM, BUT HE
WOULDN'T
LISTEN.

HE JUST
WOULDN'T
FUCKIN'
LISTEN. AND
NOW...

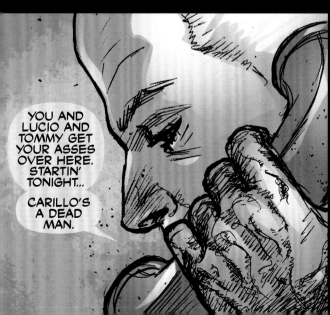

YOU AND
LUCIO AND
TOMMY GET
YOUR ASSES
OVER HERE,
STARTIN'
TONIGHT...

CARILLO'S
A DEAD
MAN.

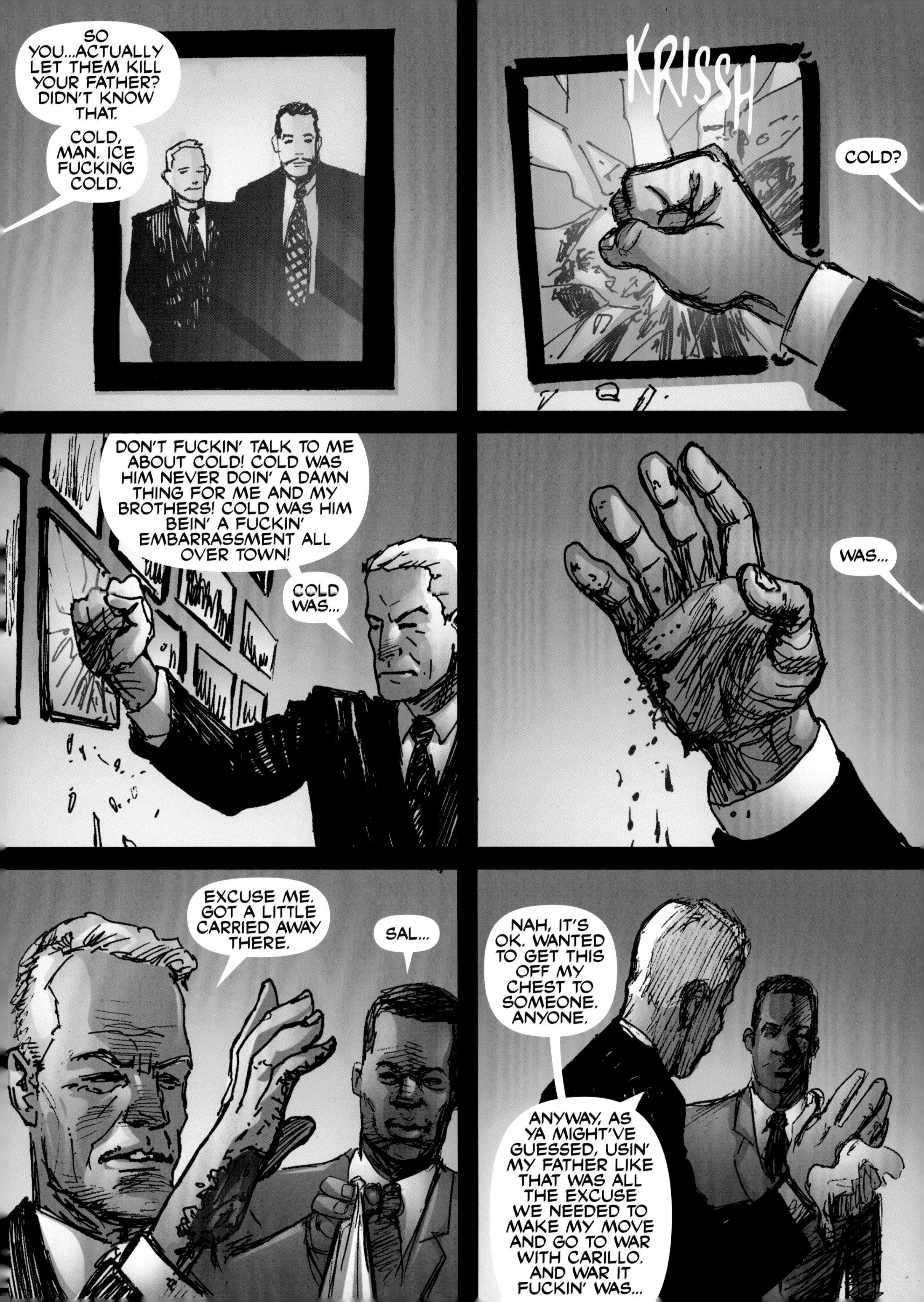
SO YOU...ACTUALLY LET THEM KILL YOUR FATHER? DIDN'T KNOW THAT.
COLD, MAN. ICE FUCKING COLD.
KRISSH
COLD?
DON'T FUCKIN' TALK TO ME ABOUT COLD! COLD WAS HIM NEVER DOIN' A DAMN THING FOR ME AND MY BROTHERS! COLD WAS HIM BEIN' A FUCKIN' EMBARRASSMENT ALL OVER TOWN!
COLD WAS...
WAS...
EXCUSE ME. GOT A LITTLE CARRIED AWAY THERE.
SAL...
NAH, IT'S OK. WANTED TO GET THIS OFF MY CHEST TO SOMEONE. ANYONE.
ANYWAY, AS YA MIGHT'VE GUESSED, USIN' MY FATHER LIKE THAT WAS ALL THE EXCUSE WE NEEDED TO MAKE MY MOVE AND GO TO WAR WITH CARILLO. AND WAR IT FUCKIN' WAS...

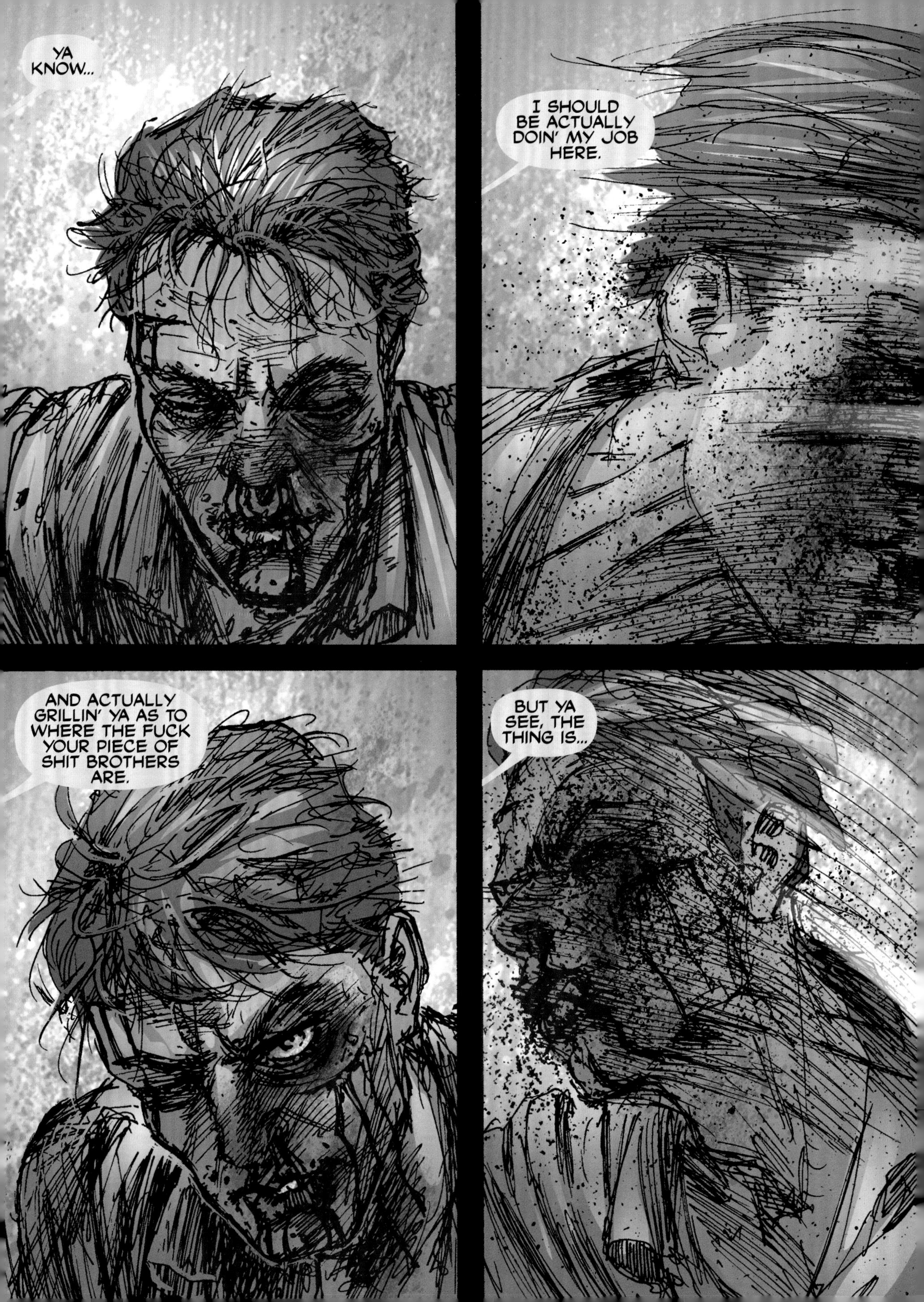

YA KNOW...
I SHOULD BE ACTUALLY DOIN' MY JOB HERE.
AND ACTUALLY GRILLIN' YA AS TO WHERE THE FUCK YOUR PIECE OF SHIT BROTHERS ARE.
BUT YA SEE, THE THING IS...

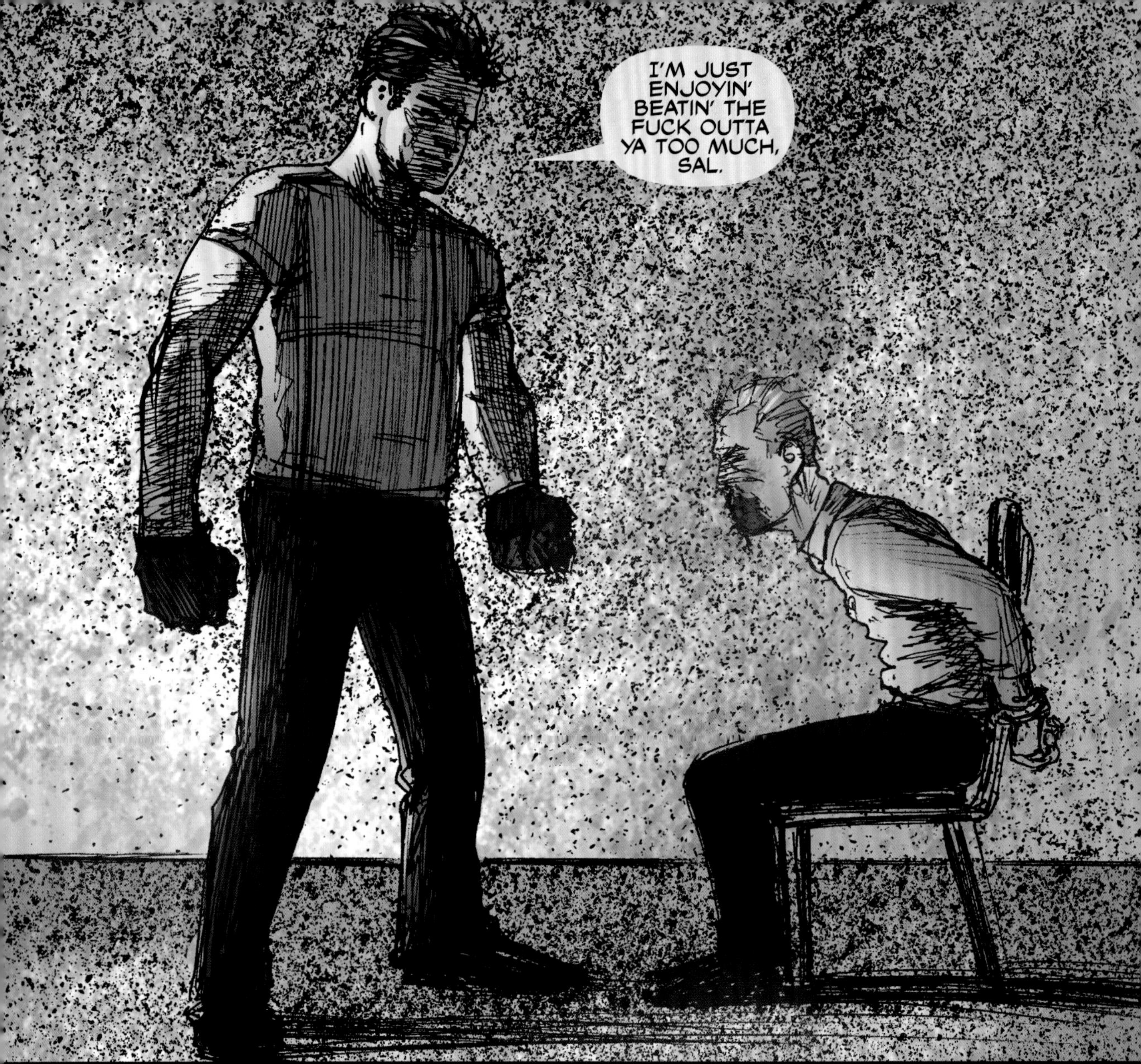
I'M JUST ENJOYIN' BEATIN' THE FUCK OUTTA YA TOO MUCH, SAL.

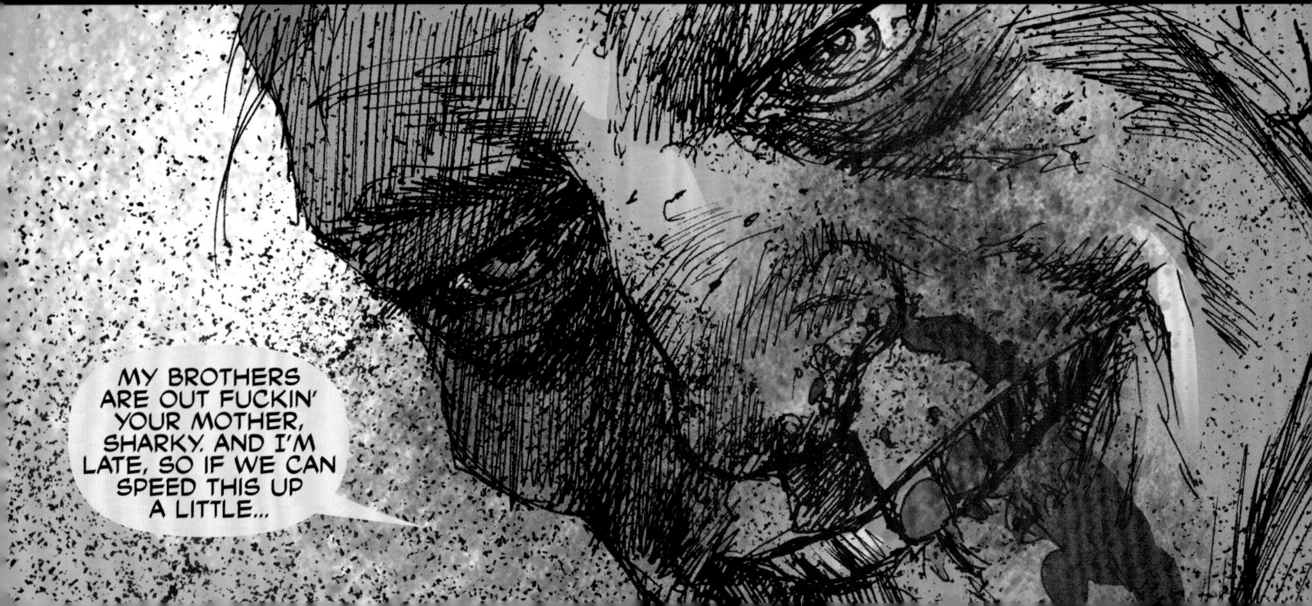
MY BROTHERS ARE OUT FUCKIN' YOUR MOTHER, SHARKY, AND I'M LATE, SO IF WE CAN SPEED THIS UP A LITTLE...

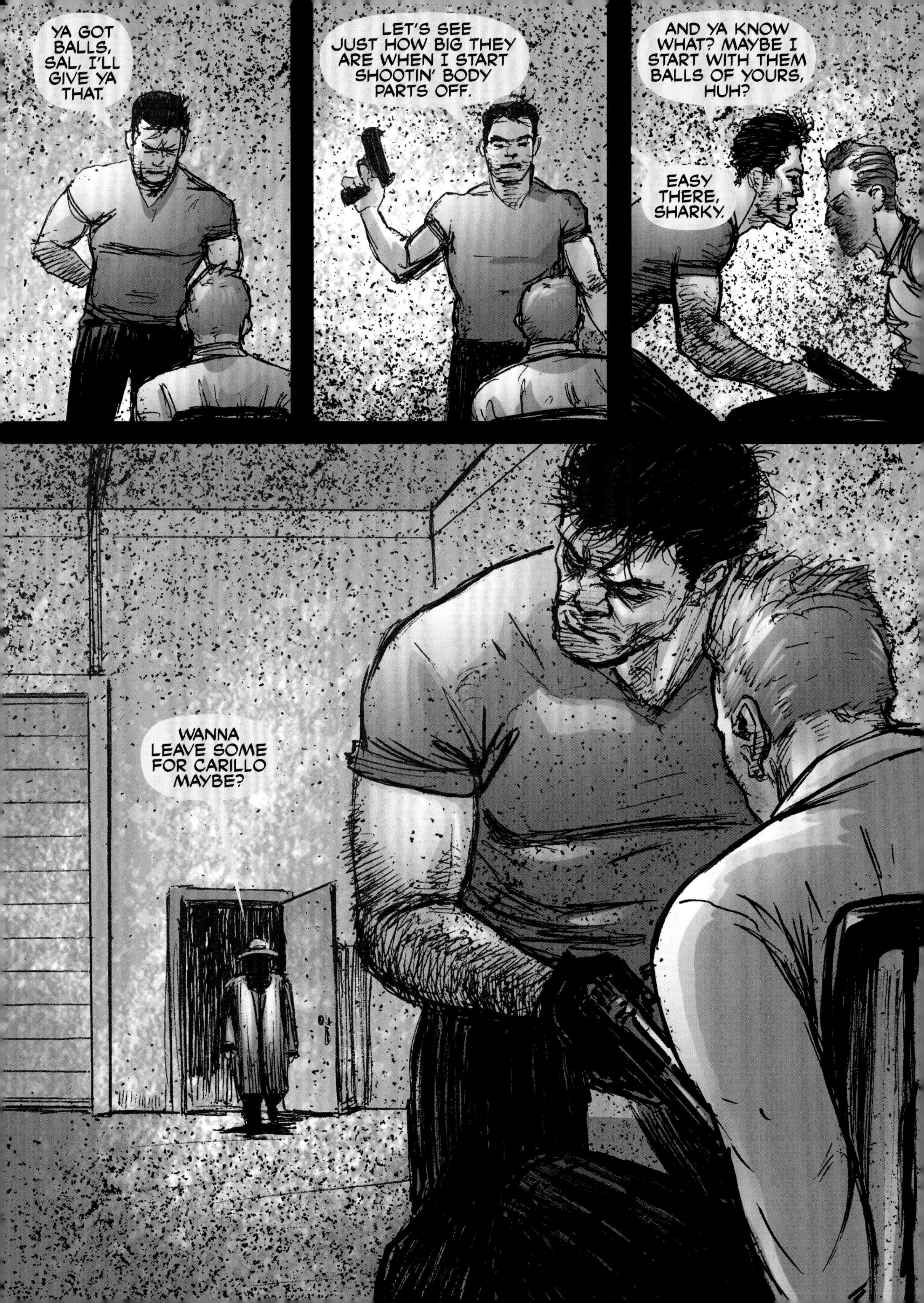
YA GOT BALLS, SAL, I'LL GIVE YA THAT.
LET'S SEE JUST HOW BIG THEY ARE WHEN I START SHOOTIN' BODY PARTS OFF.
AND YA KNOW WHAT? MAYBE I START WITH THEM BALLS OF YOURS, HUH?
EASY THERE, SHARKY.
WANNA LEAVE SOME FOR CARILLO MAYBE?

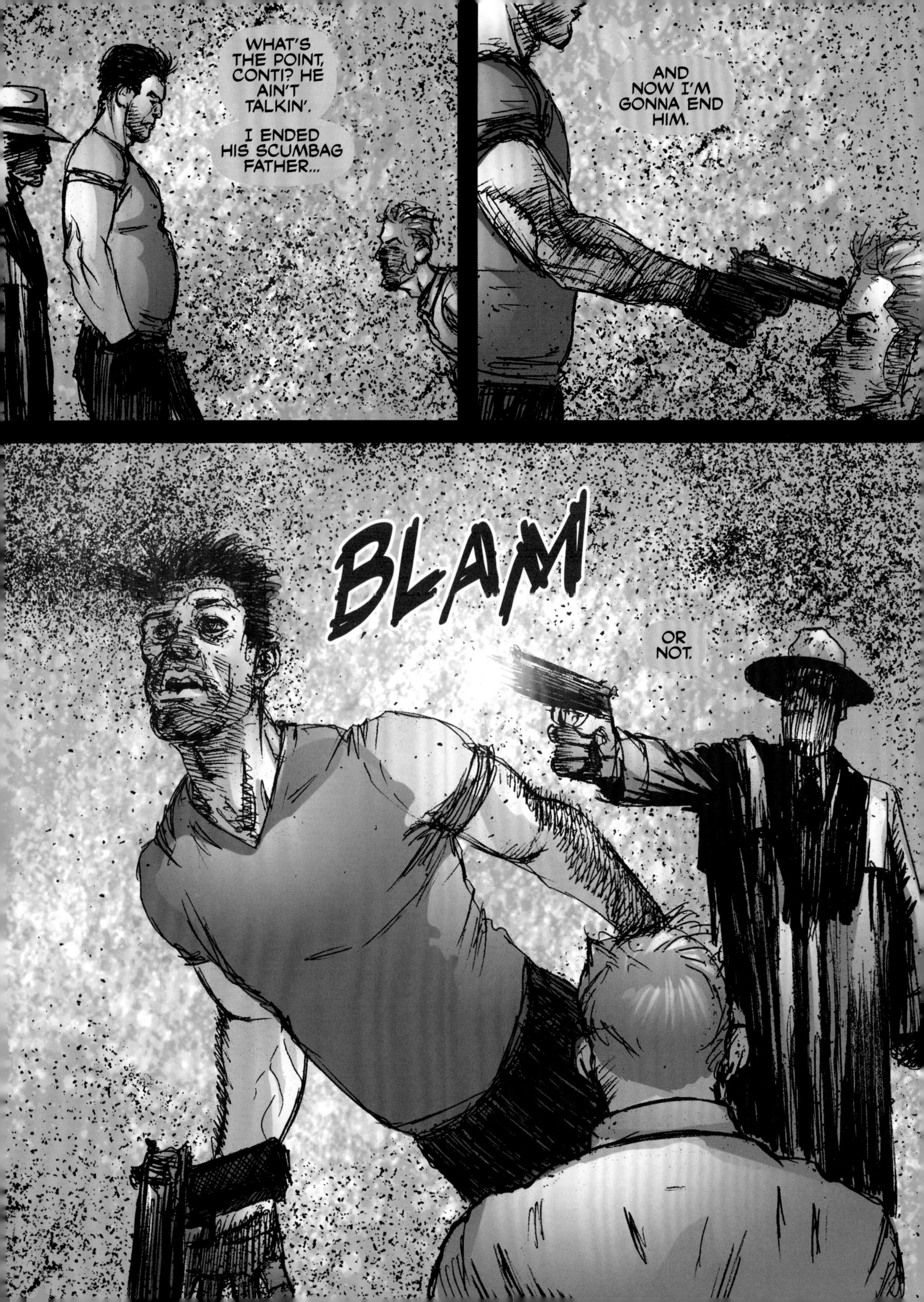
WHAT'S THE POINT, CONTI? HE AIN'T TALKIN'.
I ENDED HIS SCUMBAG FATHER...
AND NOW I'M GONNA END HIM.
BLAM
OR NOT.

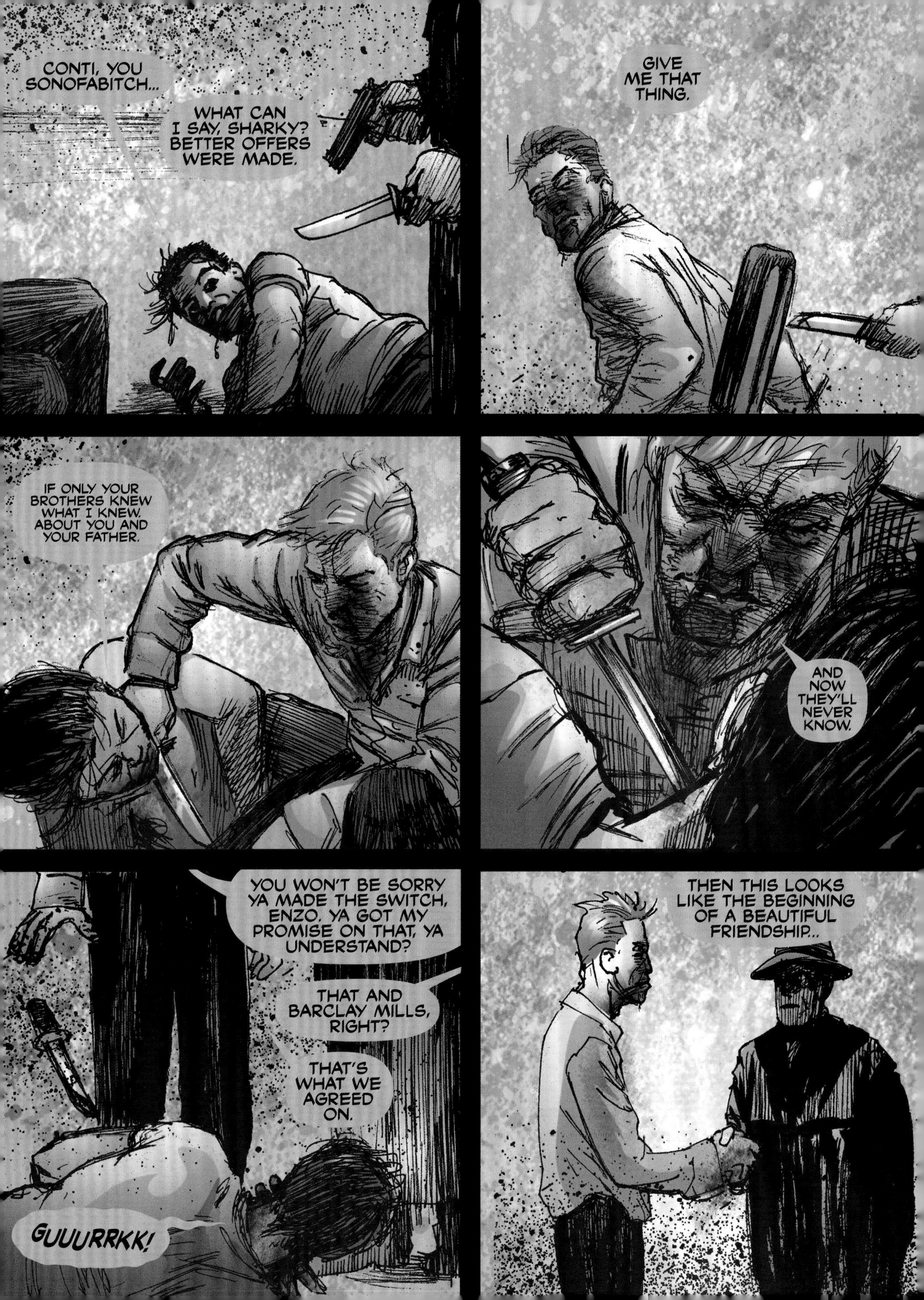
CONTI, YOU SONOFABITCH...
WHAT CAN I SAY, SHARKY? BETTER OFFERS WERE MADE.
GIVE ME THAT THING.
IF ONLY YOUR BROTHERS KNEW WHAT I KNEW. ABOUT YOU AND YOUR FATHER.
AND NOW THEY'LL NEVER KNOW.
YOU WON'T BE SORRY YA MADE THE SWITCH, ENZO. YA GOT MY PROMISE ON THAT, YA UNDERSTAND?
THAT AND BARCLAY MILLS, RIGHT?
THAT'S WHAT WE AGREED ON.
GUUURRKK!
THEN THIS LOOKS LIKE THE BEGINNING OF A BEAUTIFUL FRIENDSHIP...

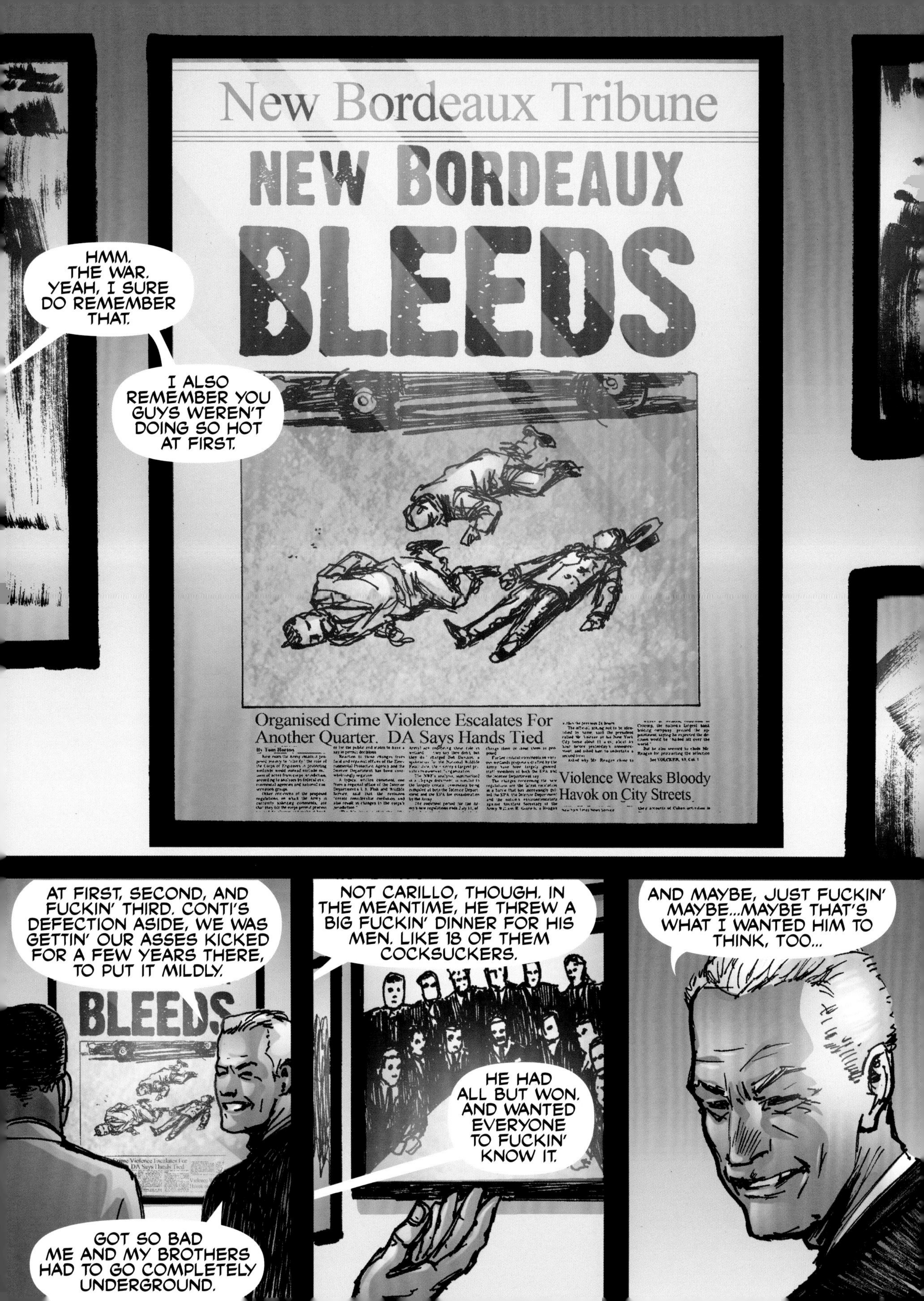

New Bordeaux Tribune
NEW BORDEAUX BLEEDS
Organised Crime Violence Escalates For Another Quarter. DA Says Hands Tied
Violence Wreaks Bloody Havok on City Streets
HMM. THE WAR. YEAH, I SURE DO REMEMBER THAT.
I ALSO REMEMBER YOU GUYS WEREN'T DOING SO HOT AT FIRST.
AT FIRST, SECOND, AND FUCKIN' THIRD. CONTI'S DEFECTION ASIDE, WE WAS GETTIN' OUR ASSES KICKED FOR A FEW YEARS THERE, TO PUT IT MILDLY.
BLEEDS
GOT SO BAD ME AND MY BROTHERS HAD TO GO COMPLETELY UNDERGROUND.
NOT CARILLO, THOUGH. IN THE MEANTIME, HE THREW A BIG FUCKIN' DINNER FOR HIS MEN. LIKE 18 OF THEM COCKSUCKERS.
HE HAD ALL BUT WON, AND WANTED EVERYONE TO FUCKIN' KNOW IT.
AND MAYBE, JUST FUCKIN' MAYBE...MAYBE THAT'S WHAT I WANTED HIM TO THINK, TOO...

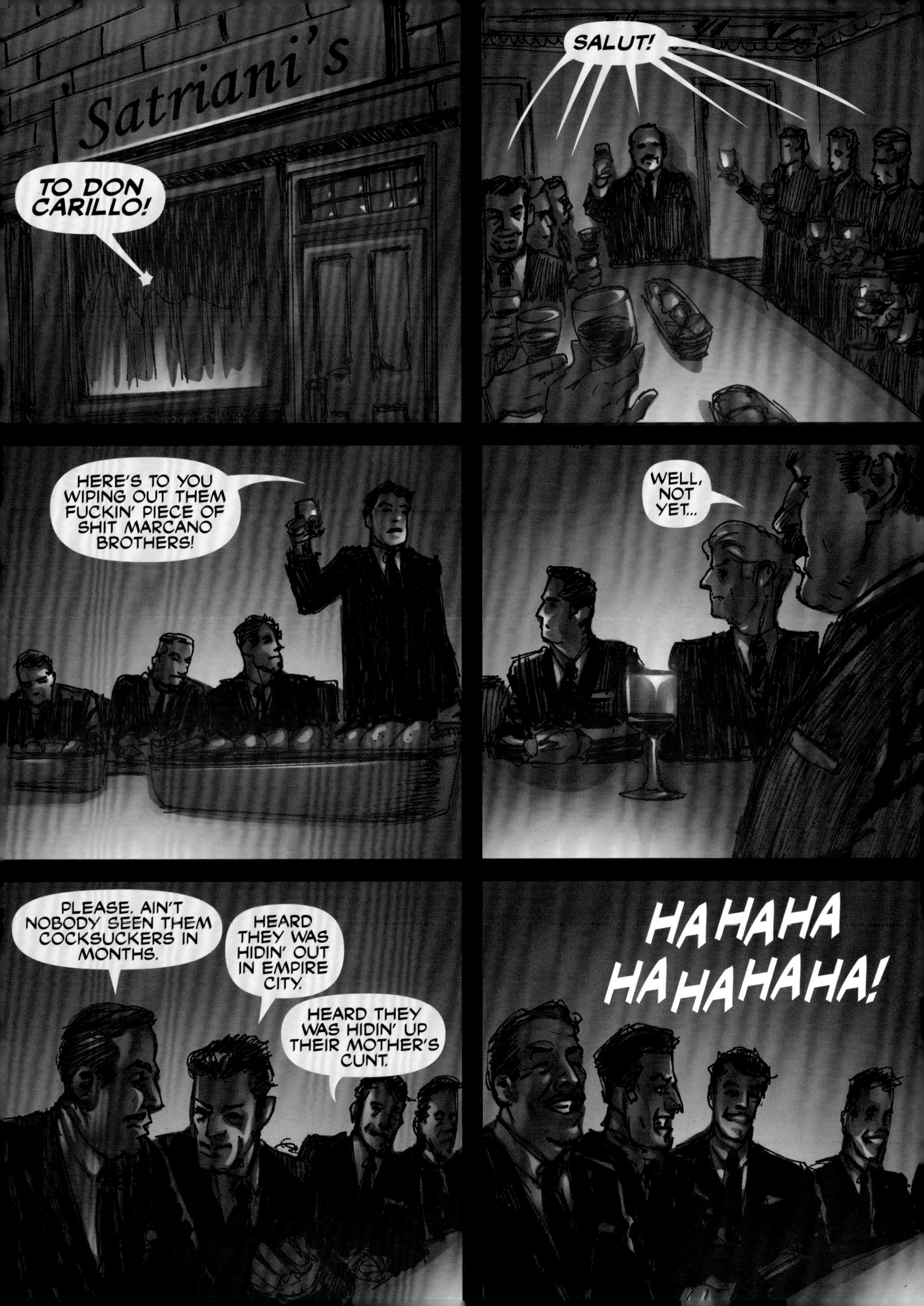
Satriani's
TO DON CARILLO!
SALUT!
HERE'S TO YOU WIPING OUT THEM FUCKIN' PIECE OF SHIT MARCANO BROTHERS!
WELL, NOT YET...
PLEASE. AIN'T NOBODY SEEN THEM COCKSUCKERS IN MONTHS.
HEARD THEY WAS HIDIN' OUT IN EMPIRE CITY.
HEARD THEY WAS HIDIN' UP THEIR MOTHER'S CUNT.
HAHAHA HAHAHAHAHA!

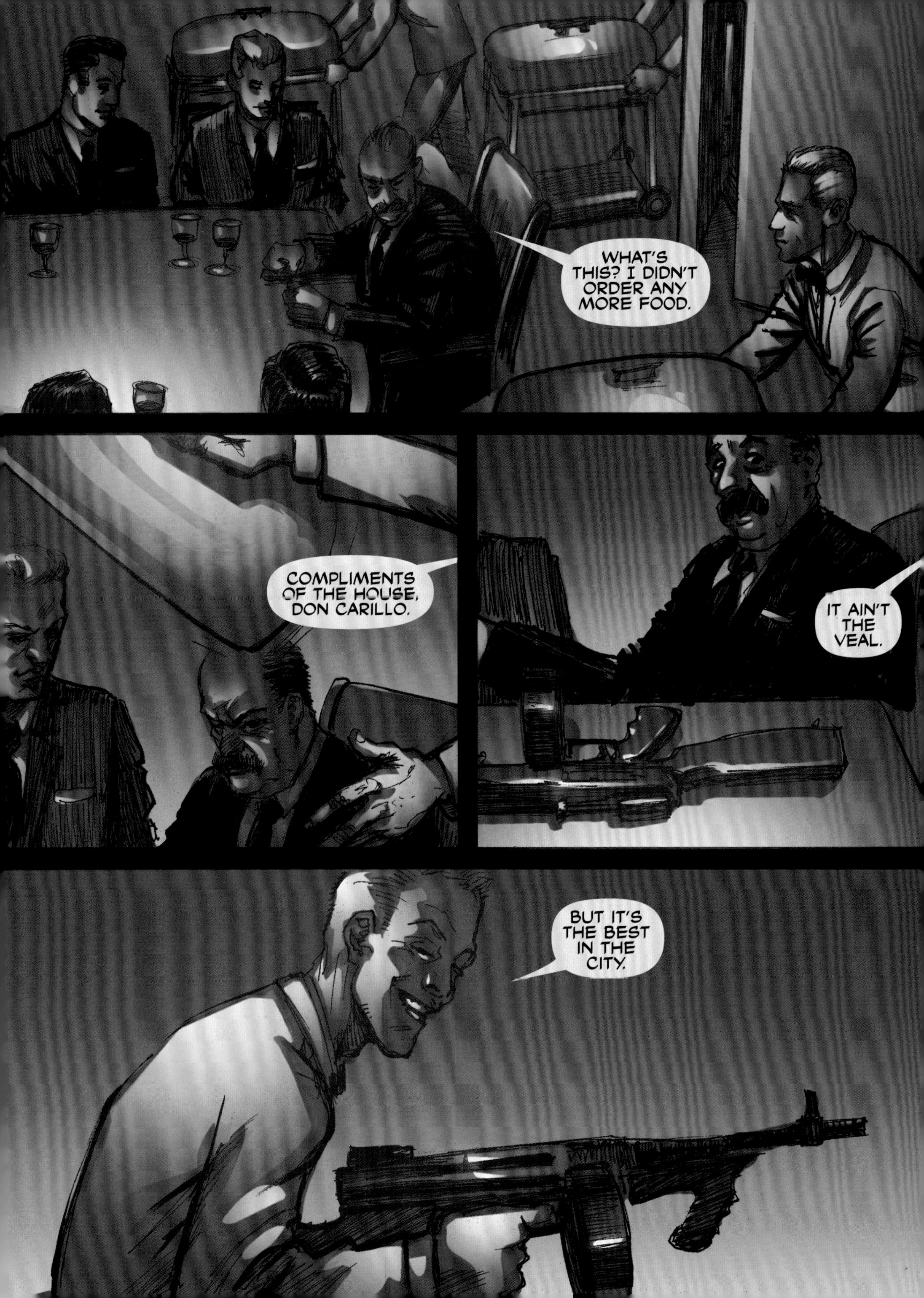
WHAT'S THIS? I DIDN'T ORDER ANY MORE FOOD.
COMPLIMENTS OF THE HOUSE, DON CARILLO.
IT AIN'T THE VEAL.
BUT IT'S THE BEST IN THE CITY.

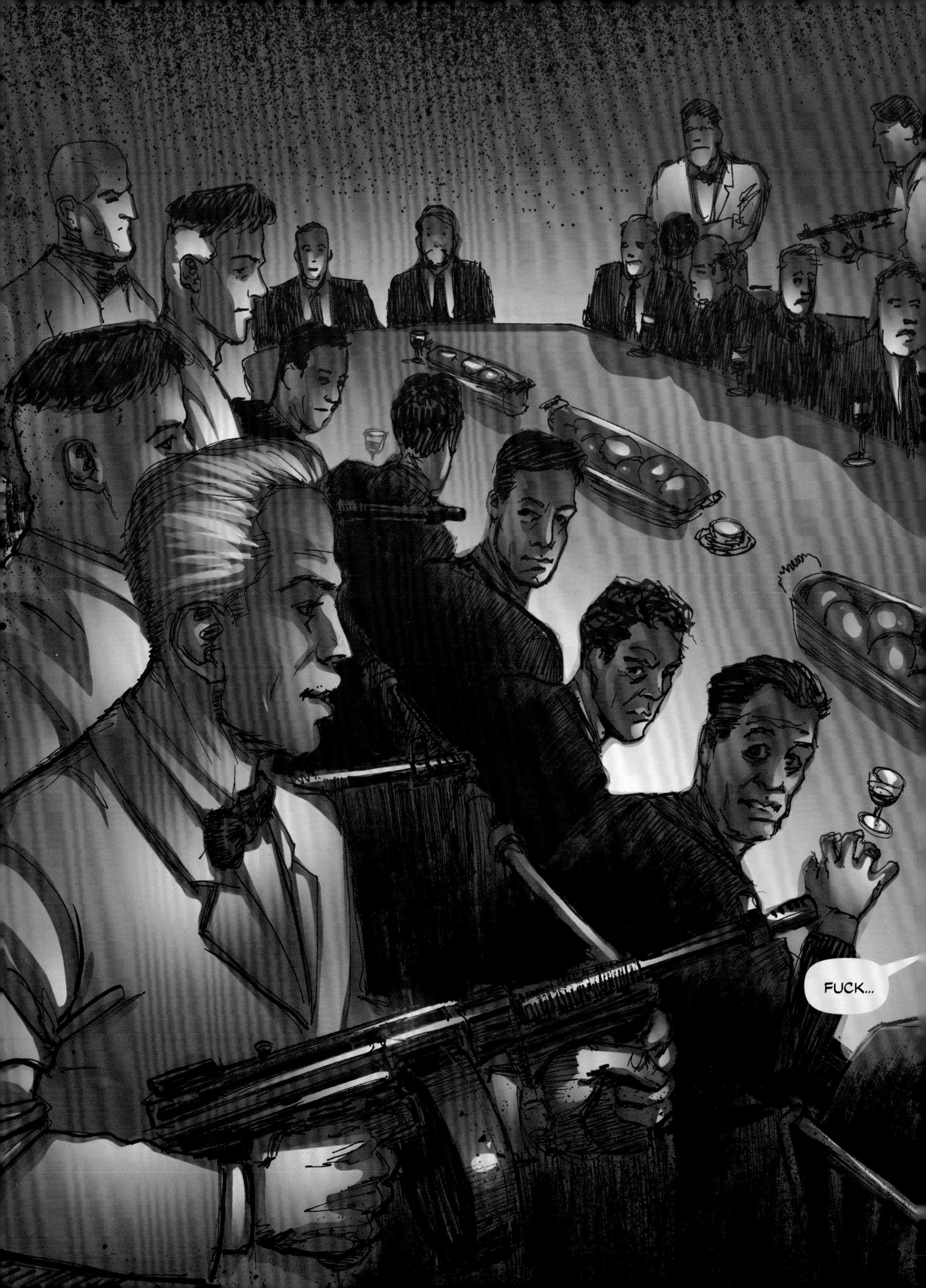
FUCK...

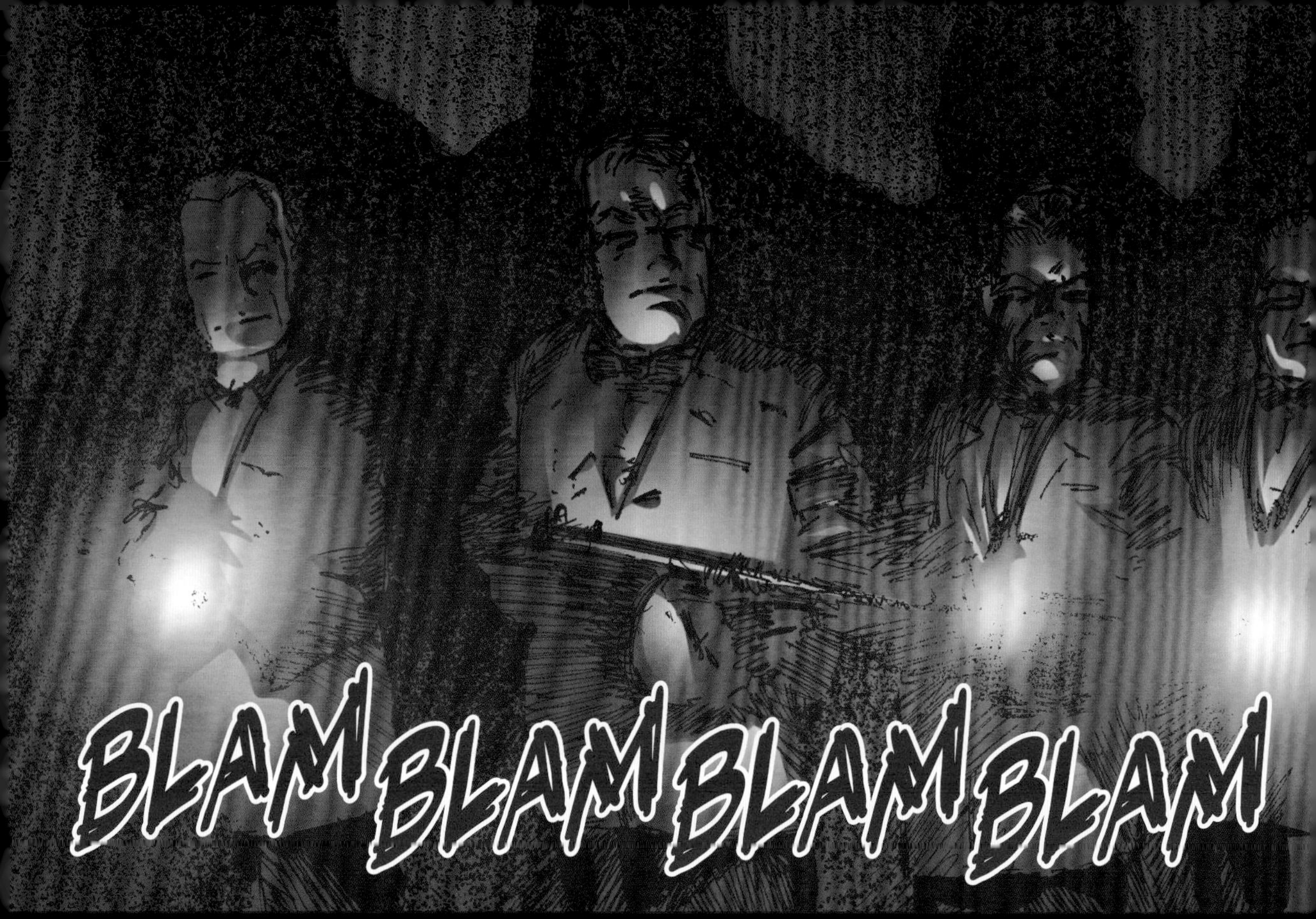
BLAM BLAM BLAM BLAM
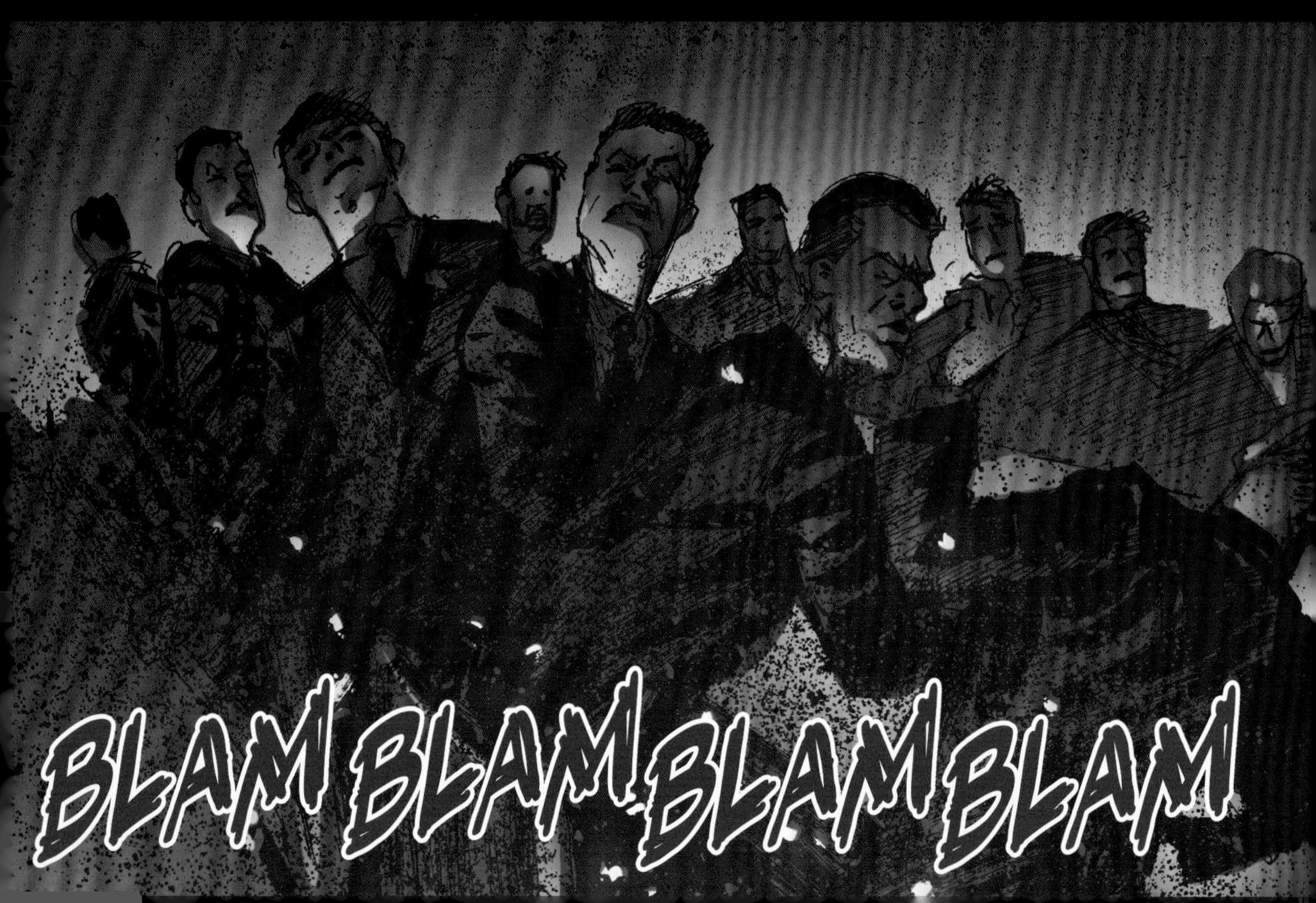
BLAM BLAM BLAM BLAM

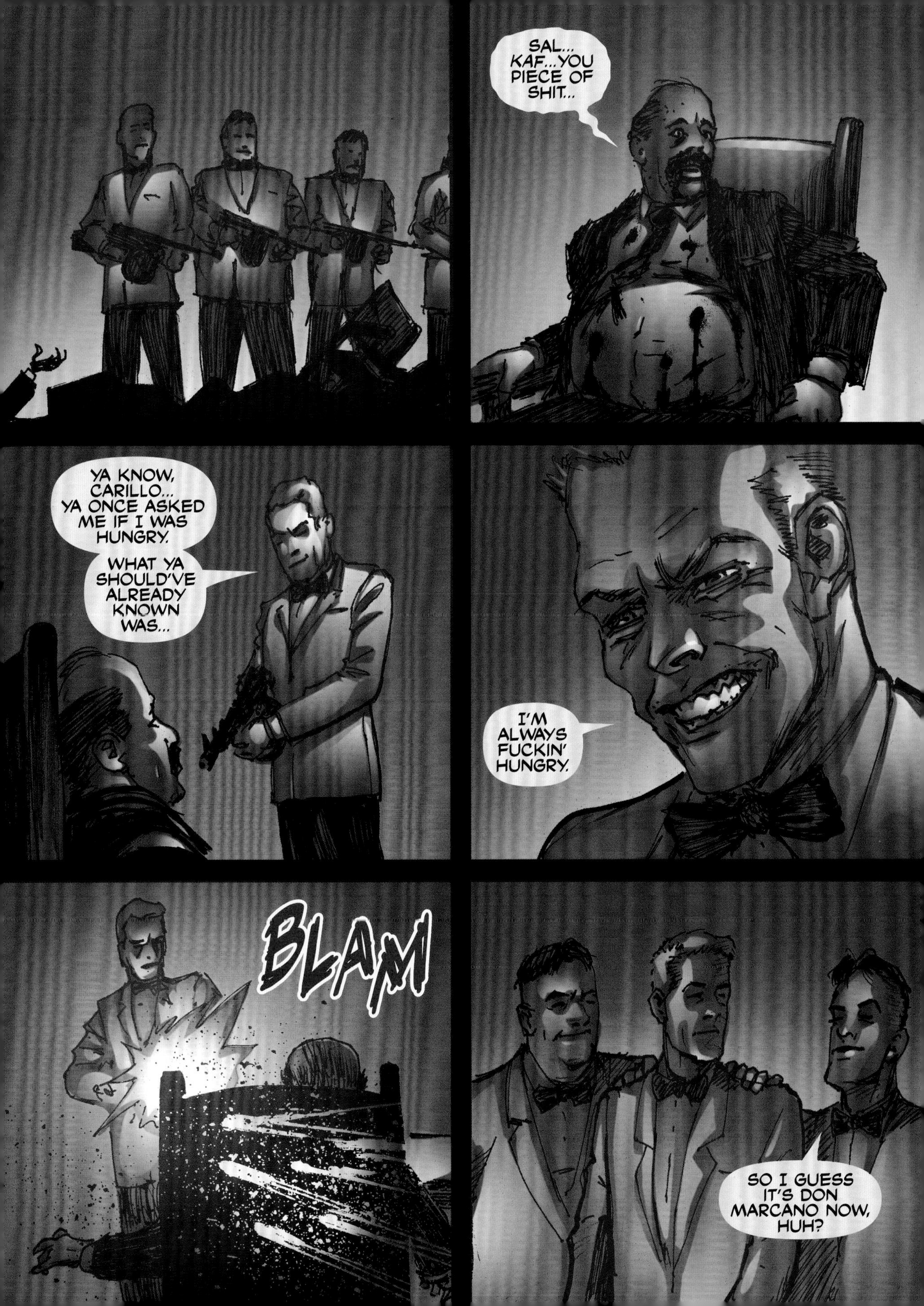
SAL... KAF...YOU PIECE OF SHIT...
YA KNOW, CARILLO... YA ONCE ASKED ME IF I WAS HUNGRY.
WHAT YA SHOULD'VE ALREADY KNOWN WAS...
I'M ALWAYS FUCKIN' HUNGRY.
BLAM
SO I GUESS IT'S DON MARCANO NOW, HUH?

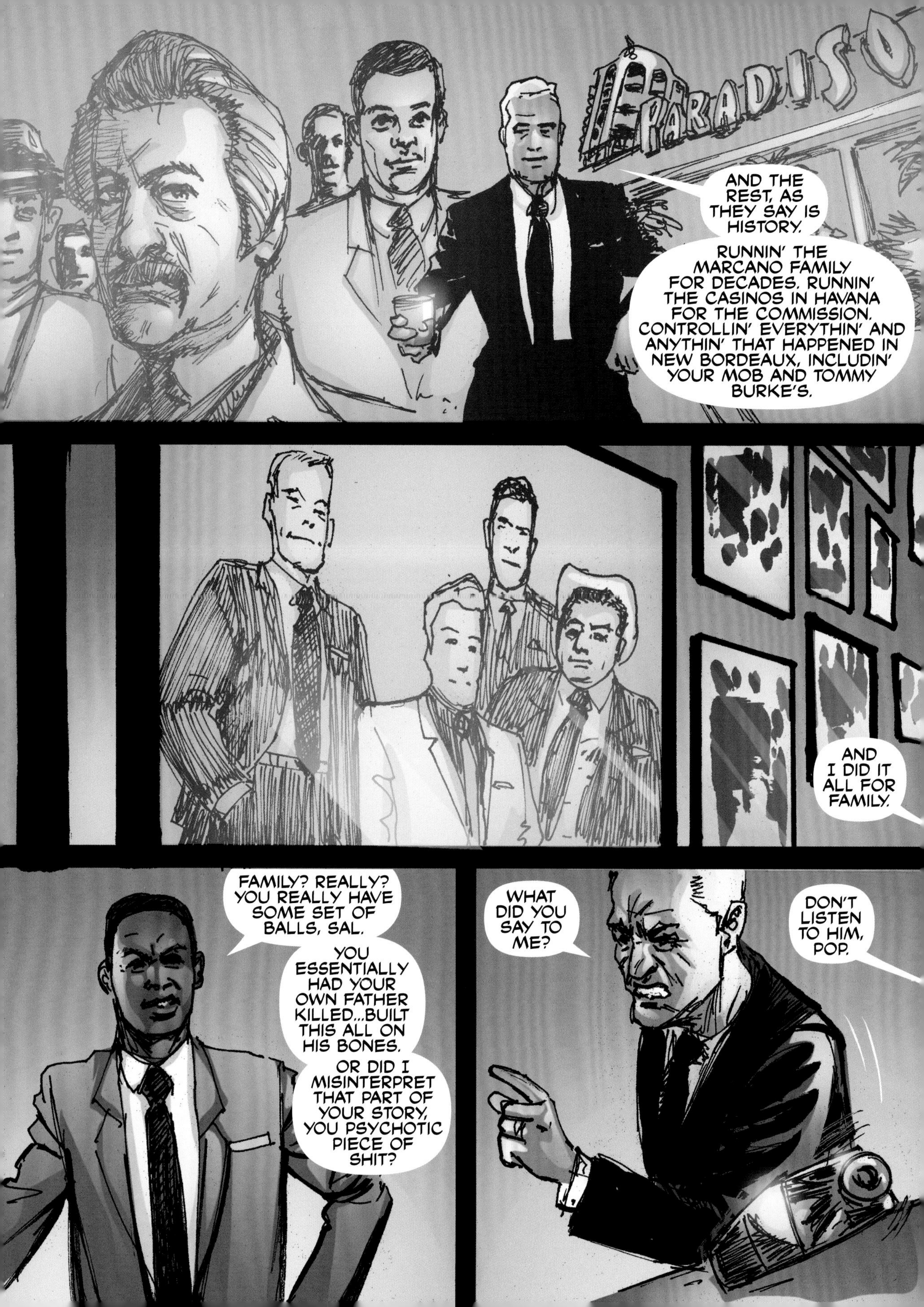
PARADISO
AND THE REST, AS THEY SAY IS HISTORY.
RUNNIN' THE MARCANO FAMILY FOR DECADES. RUNNIN' THE CASINOS IN HAVANA FOR THE COMMISSION. CONTROLLIN' EVERYTHIN' AND ANYTHIN' THAT HAPPENED IN NEW BORDEAUX, INCLUDIN' YOUR MOB AND TOMMY BURKE'S.
AND I DID IT ALL FOR FAMILY.
FAMILY? REALLY? YOU REALLY HAVE SOME SET OF BALLS, SAL.
YOU ESSENTIALLY HAD YOUR OWN FATHER KILLED...BUILT THIS ALL ON HIS BONES.
OR DID I MISINTERPRET THAT PART OF YOUR STORY, YOU PSYCHOTIC PIECE OF SHIT?
WHAT DID YOU SAY TO ME?
DON'T LISTEN TO HIM, POP.

I KNOW YA DID IT ALL FOR ME.

GIORGI!

YA KNOW I DID, SON. YA KNOW I DID. THAT'S WHY I BUILT THE CASINO, WANTED TO MAKE IT LEGIT FOR YA.

IT'S WHY I FOUGHT SO HARD AGAINST LINCOLN...

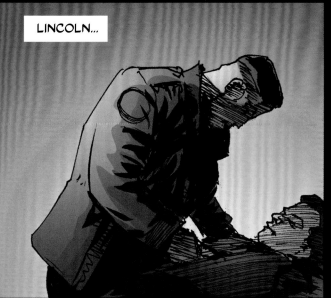

LINCOLN...

YA DID IT FOR US, TOO, RIGHT, SAL?

TOMMY, LUCIO, LOU...

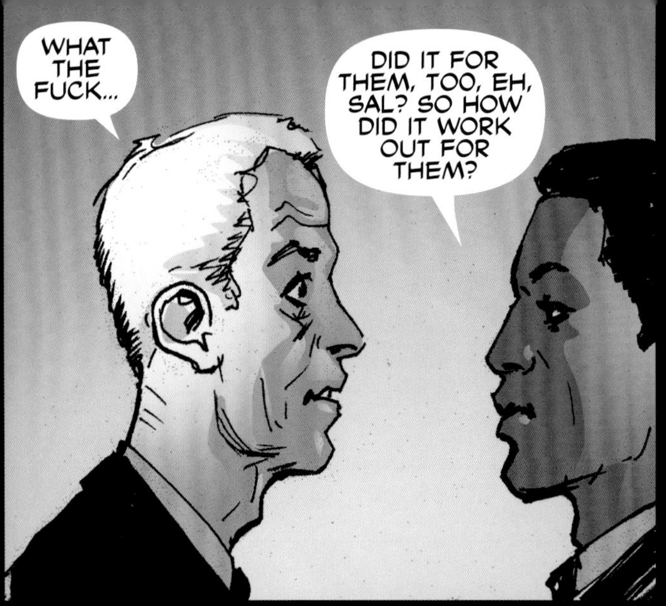
WHAT THE FUCK...
DID IT FOR THEM, TOO, EH, SAL? SO HOW DID IT WORK OUT FOR THEM?

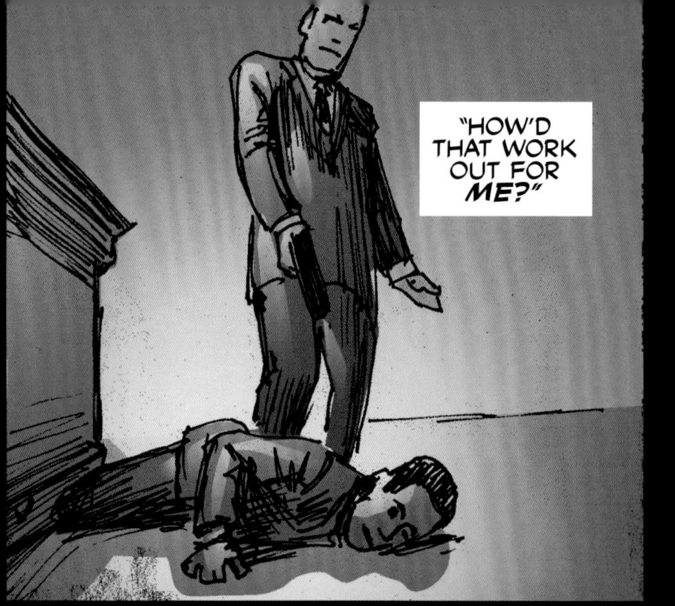
"HOW'D THAT WORK OUT FOR *ME?*"

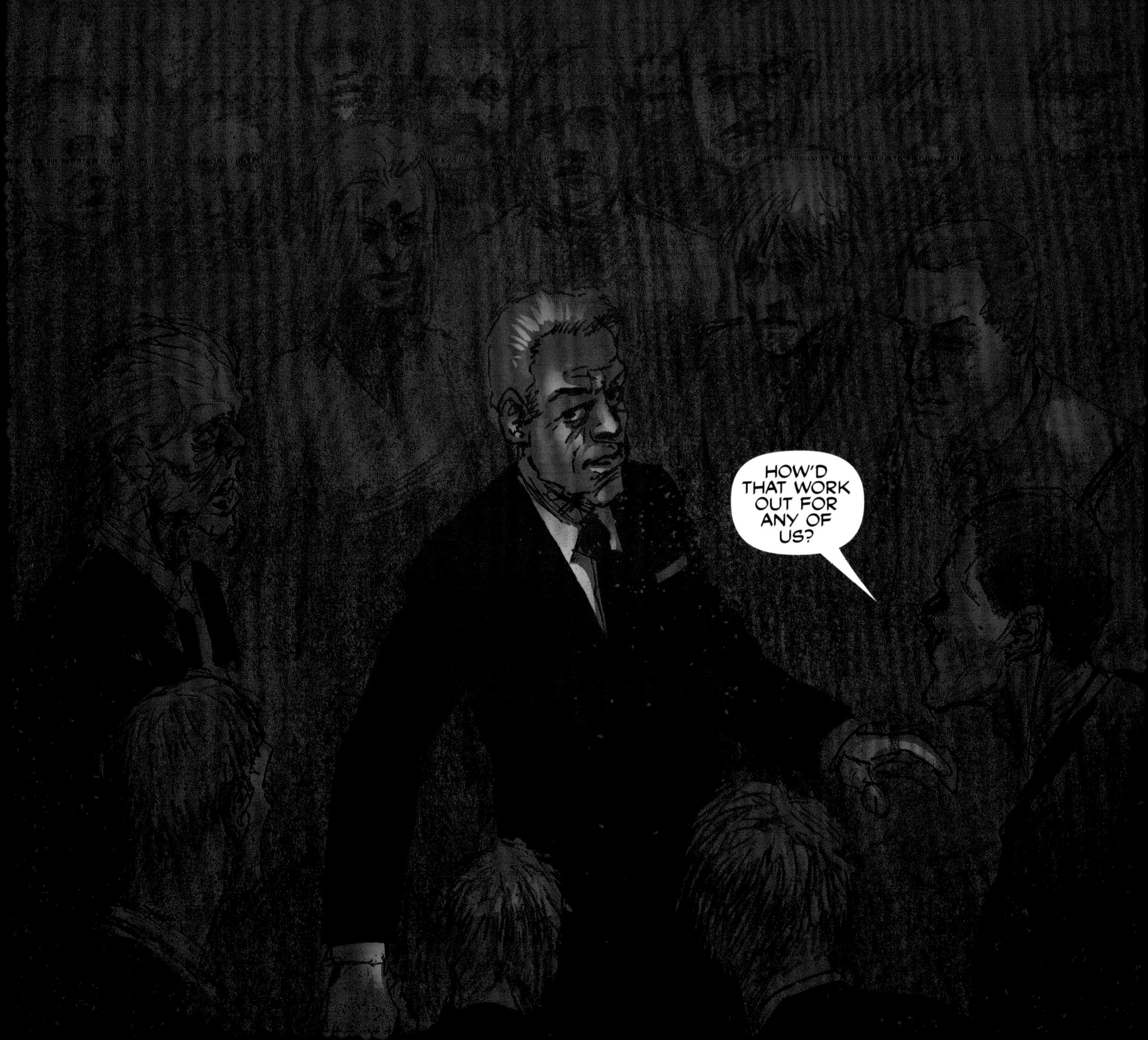
HOW'D THAT WORK OUT FOR ANY OF US?

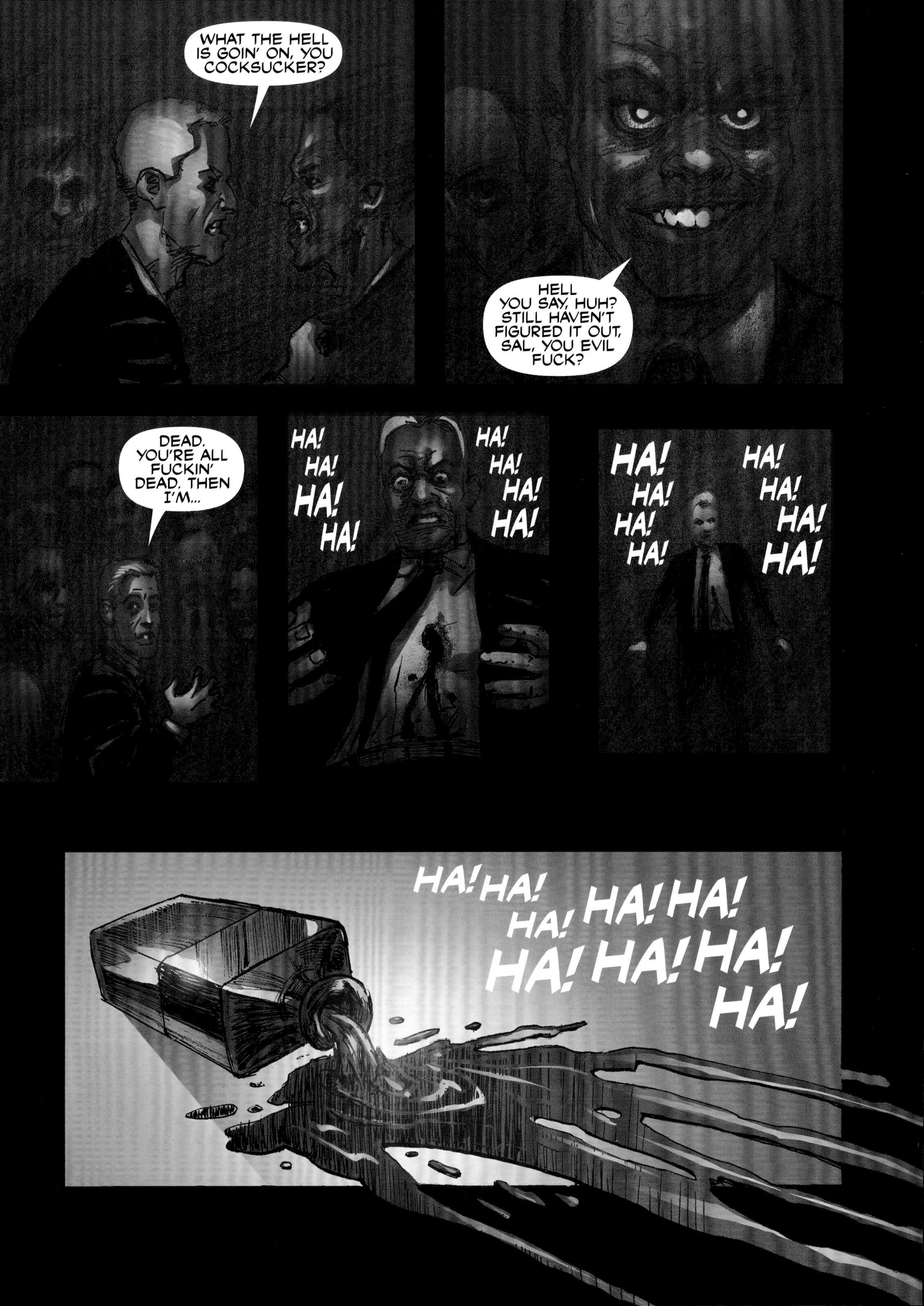
WHAT THE HELL IS GOIN' ON, YOU COCKSUCKER?
HELL YOU SAY, HUH? STILL HAVEN'T FIGURED IT OUT, SAL, YOU EVIL FUCK?
DEAD. YOU'RE ALL FUCKIN' DEAD. THEN I'M...
HA! HA! HA! HA!
HA! HA! HA! HA!
HA! HA! HA! HA!
HA! HA! HA! HA!
HA! HA! HA! HA! HA! HA! HA! HA! HA!

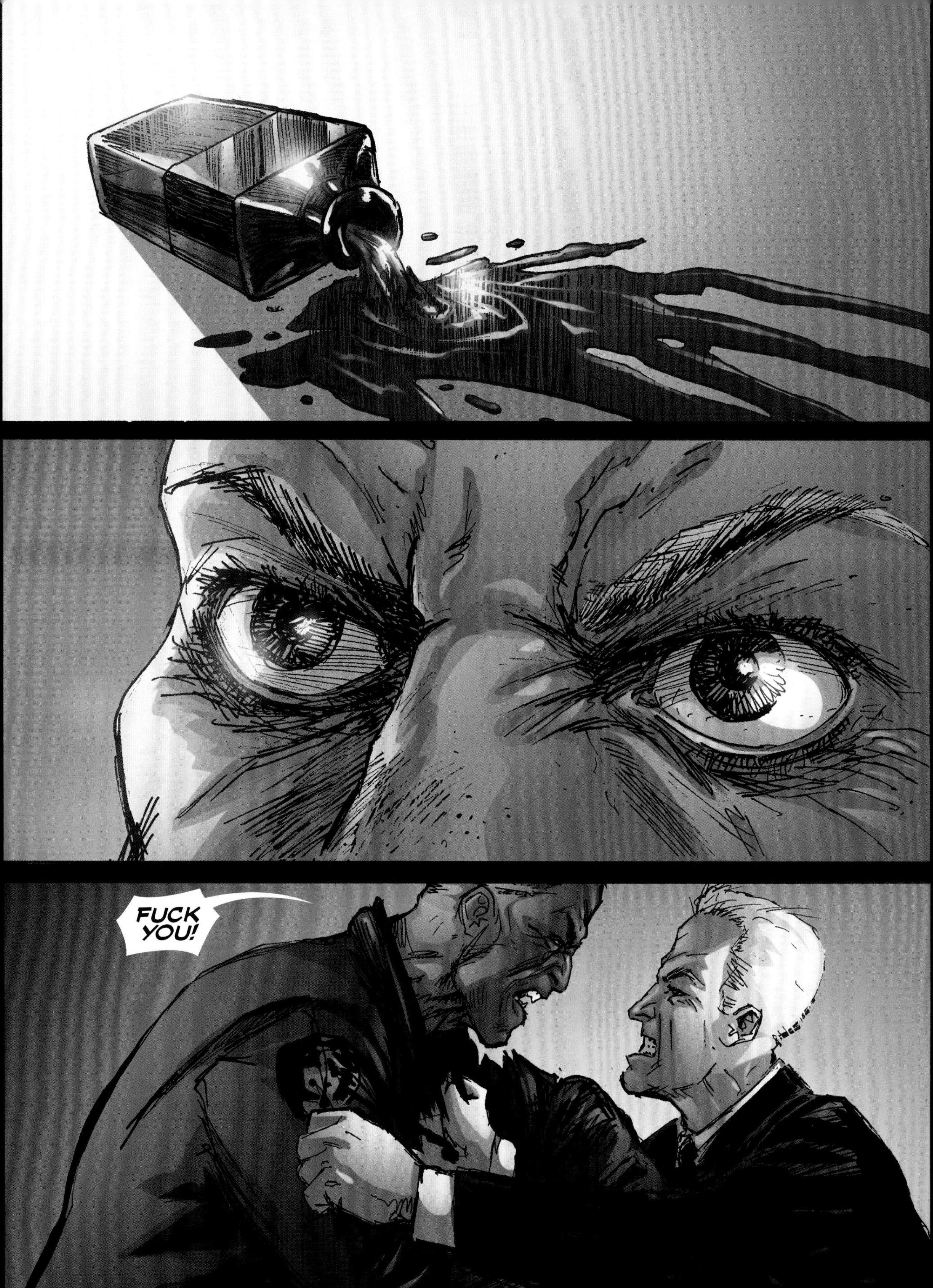
FUCK YOU!

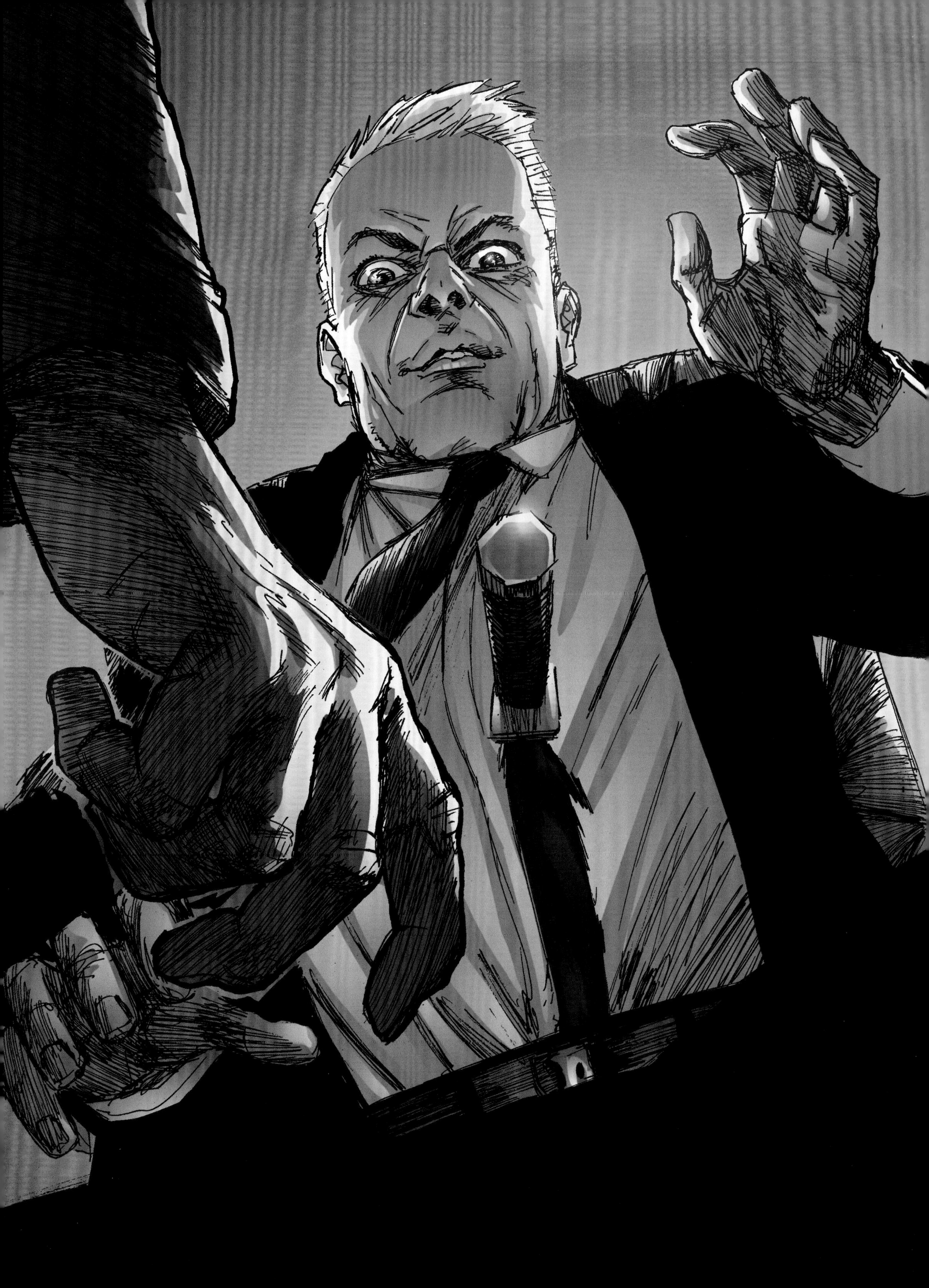

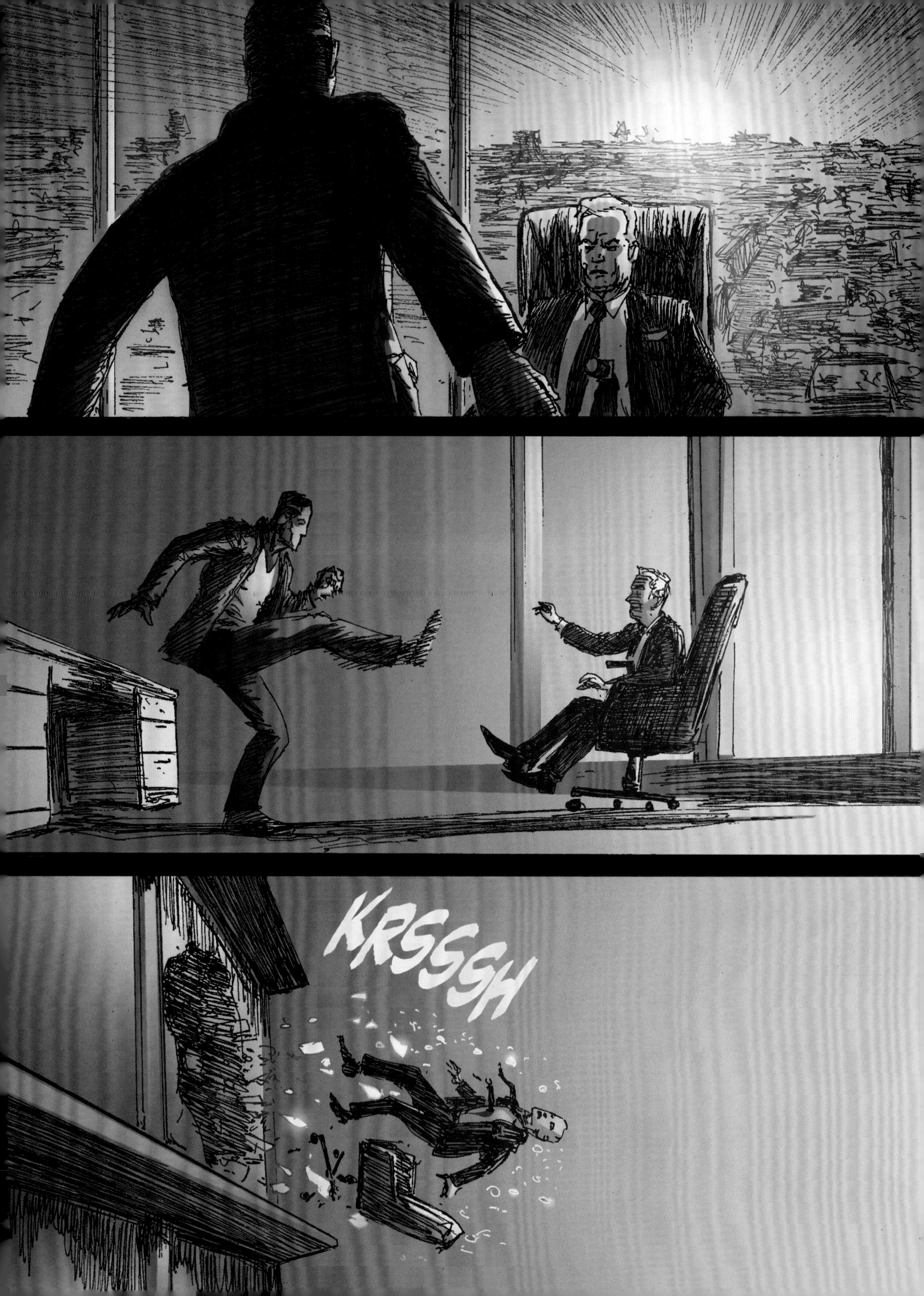
KRSSSH

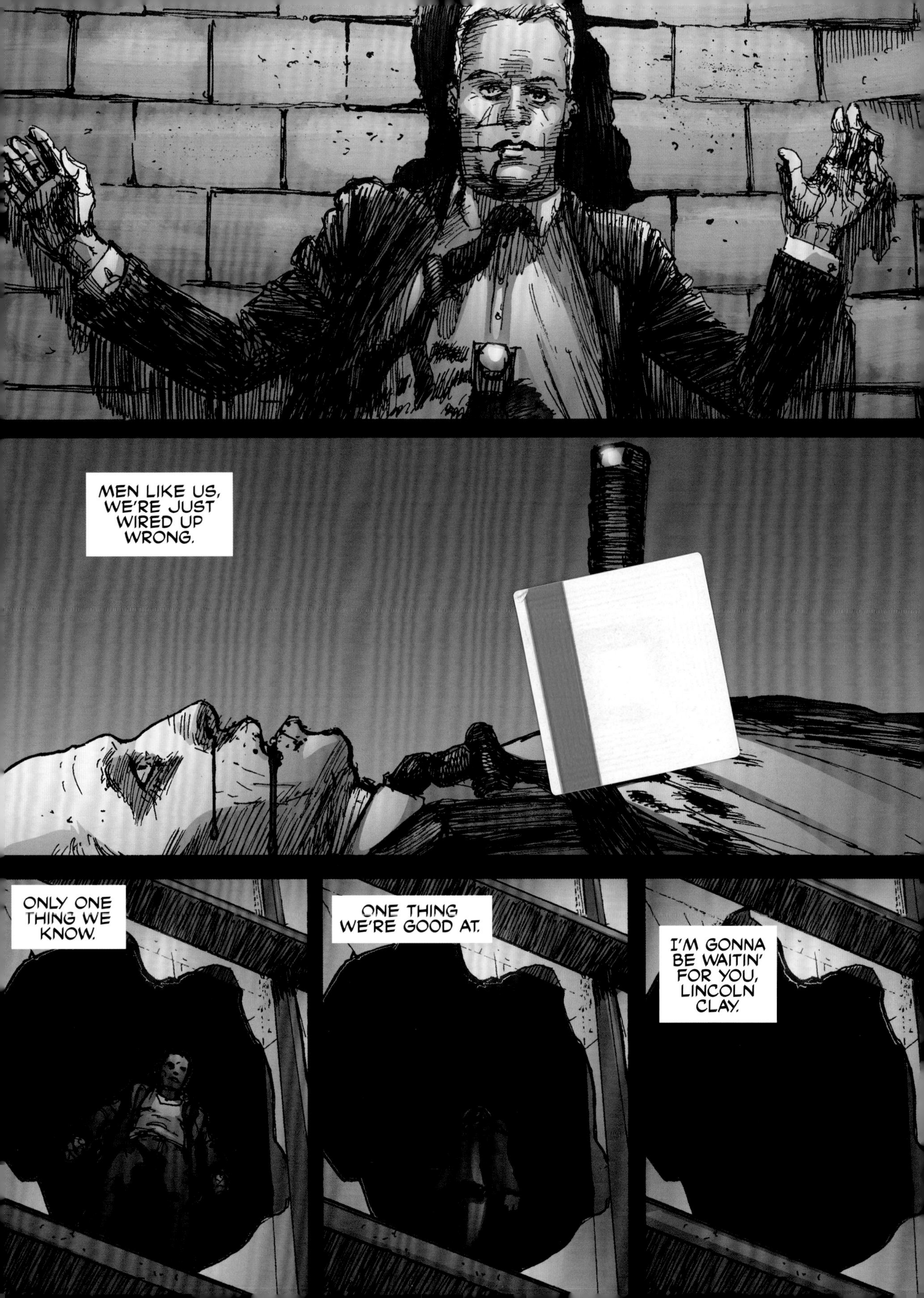
MEN LIKE US, WE'RE JUST WIRED UP WRONG.
ONLY ONE THING WE KNOW.
ONE THING WE'RE GOOD AT.
I'M GONNA BE WAITIN' FOR YOU, LINCOLN CLAY.

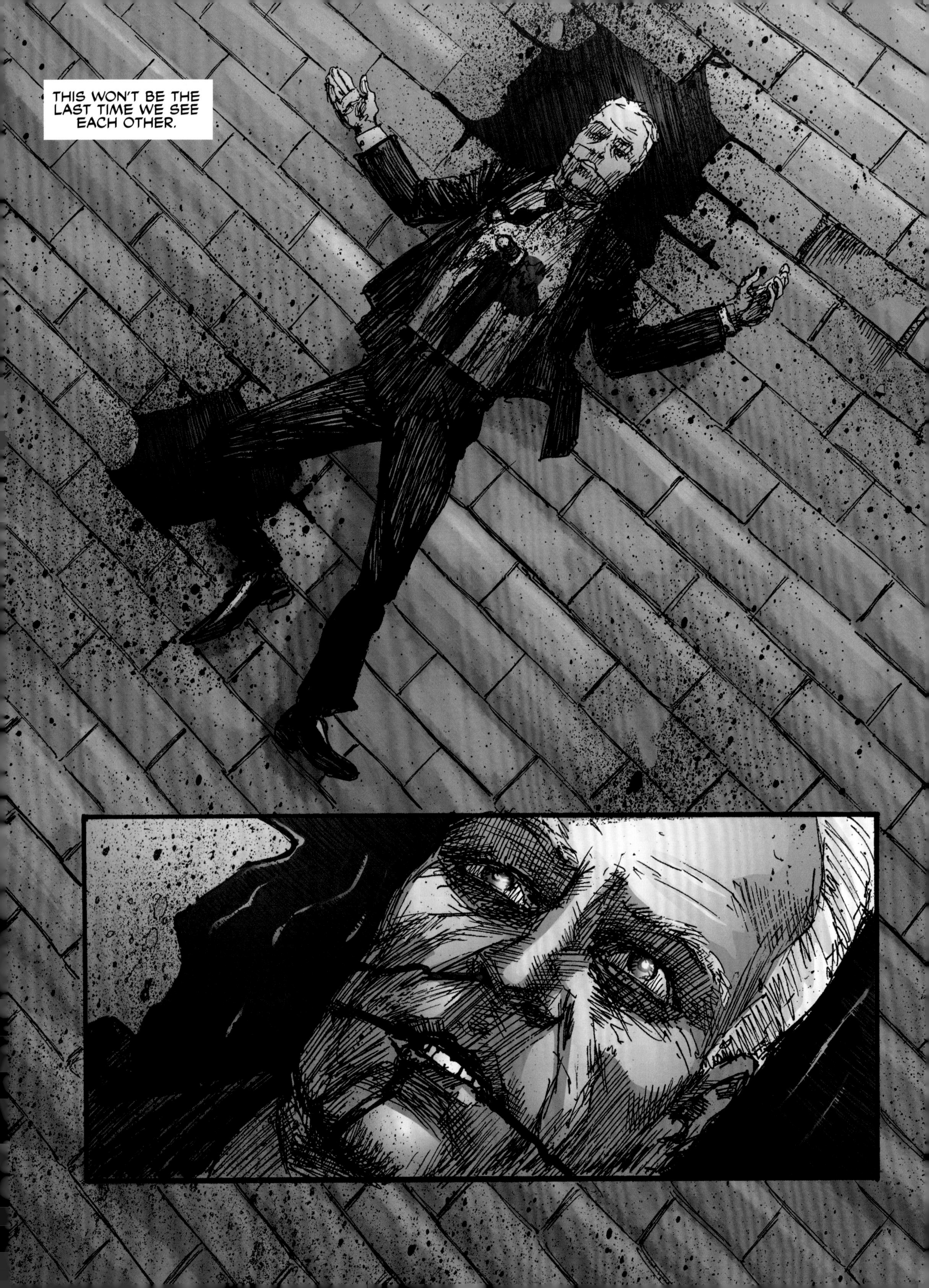
THIS WON'T BE THE LAST TIME WE SEE EACH OTHER.

Frank Tieri has written comics for Marvel, DC, and Image, and is well known for his gritty portrayal of criminals and lowlifes. Some of his titles include *New Excalibur, Iron Man, Wolverine, Weapon X, Underworld*, a post–"Avengers Disassembled" *Hercules* miniseries, *Wolverine/Darkness, X-Men: Dracula vs. Apocalypse, Civil War: War Crimes*, and *World War Hulk: Gamma Corps*.

Richard Pace, who has been an artist for *Hellboy, Batman*, and many more, resides in Toronto, smokes good cigars, and only works on the finest comics stories.

Peter Pantazis has been a professional color artist for more than twenty years. Having studied illustration at F.I.T. in New York, he moved to California to pursue a career in comic books.

He honed his craft as a member of the Wildstorm FX team for three years, and from there he has been painting/coloring and illustrating projects for companies such as Marvel Comics, DC Entertainment, Image Comics, and many other amazing publishers.

The Making of *Mafia III: The Rise And Fall Of Sal Marcano*

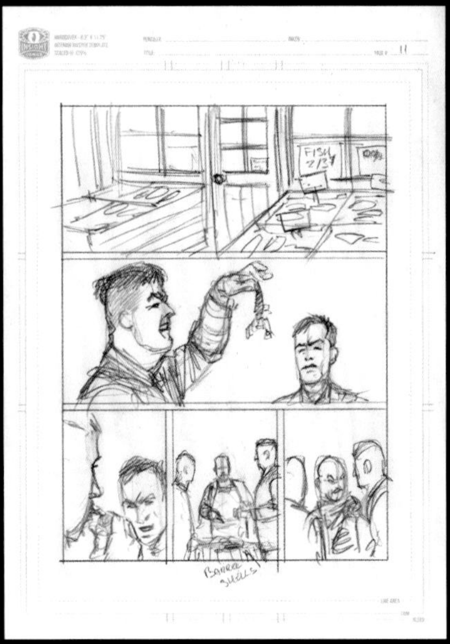

Layout Sketches
Page 15
Art by Richard Pace

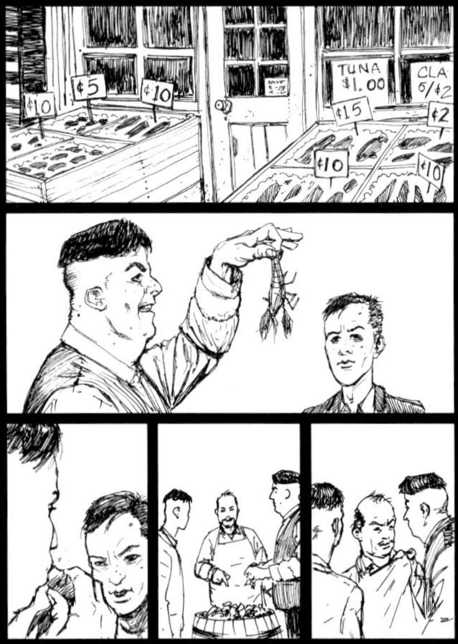
TUNA
$1.00

Inks
Page 15
Art by Richard Pace

Colors
Page 15
Colors by Peter Pantazis

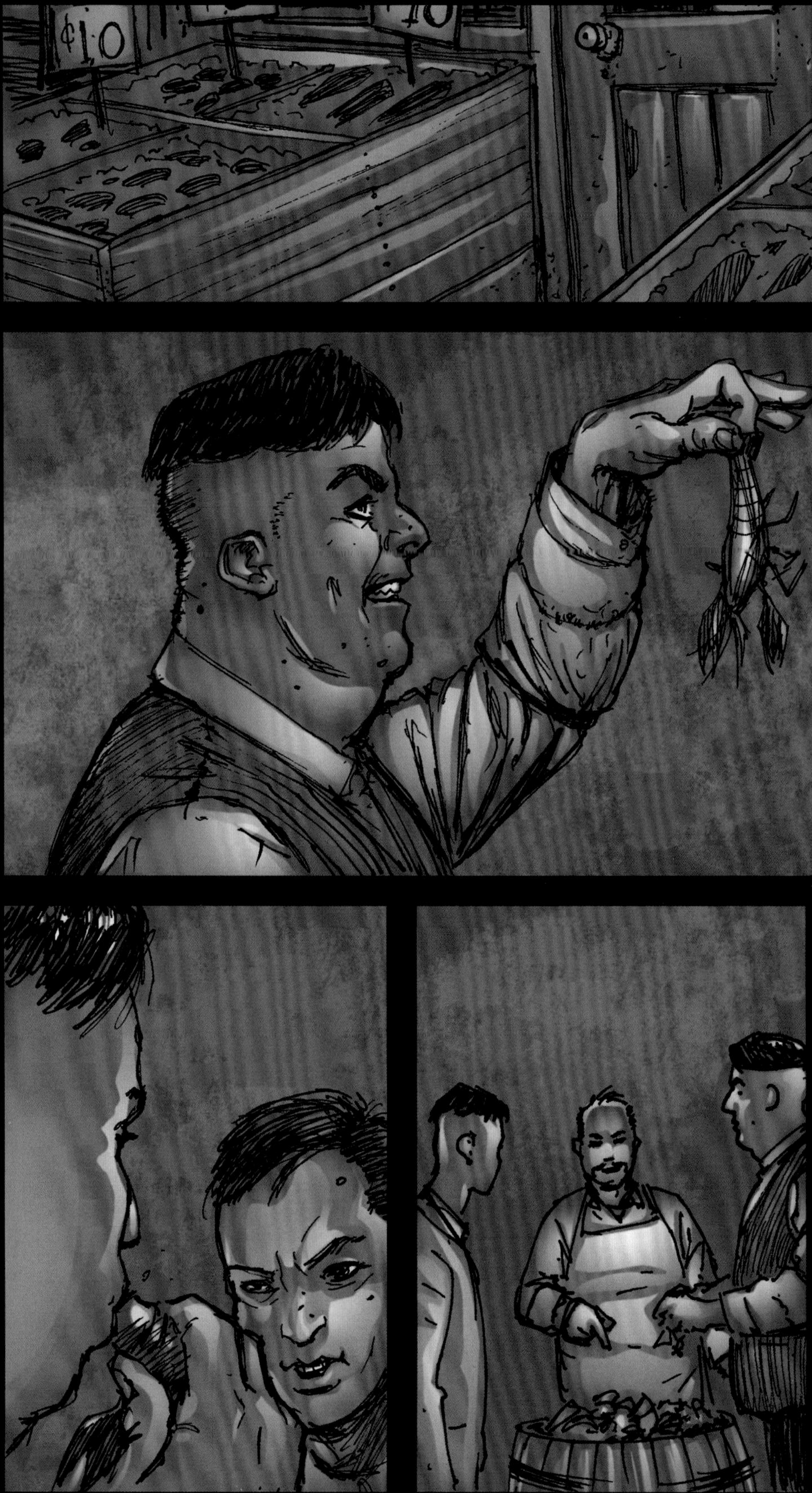

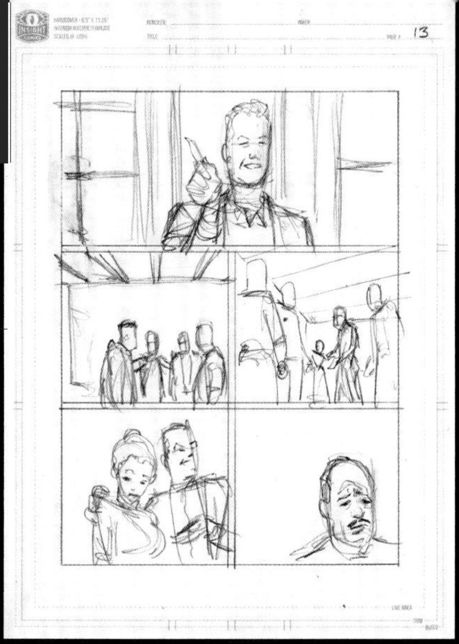

Layout Sketches
Page 17
Art by Richard Pace

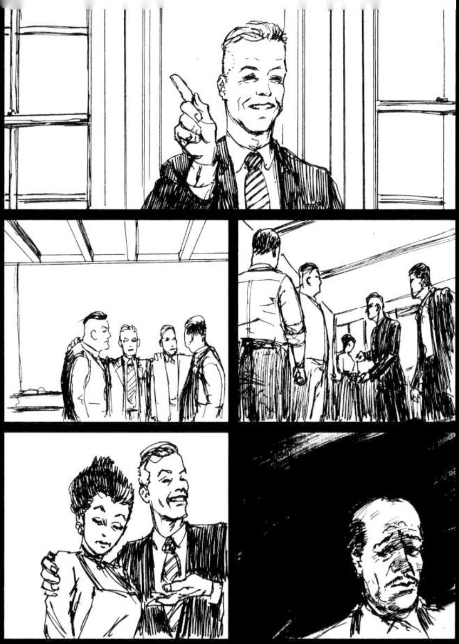

Inks
Page 17
Art by Richard Pace

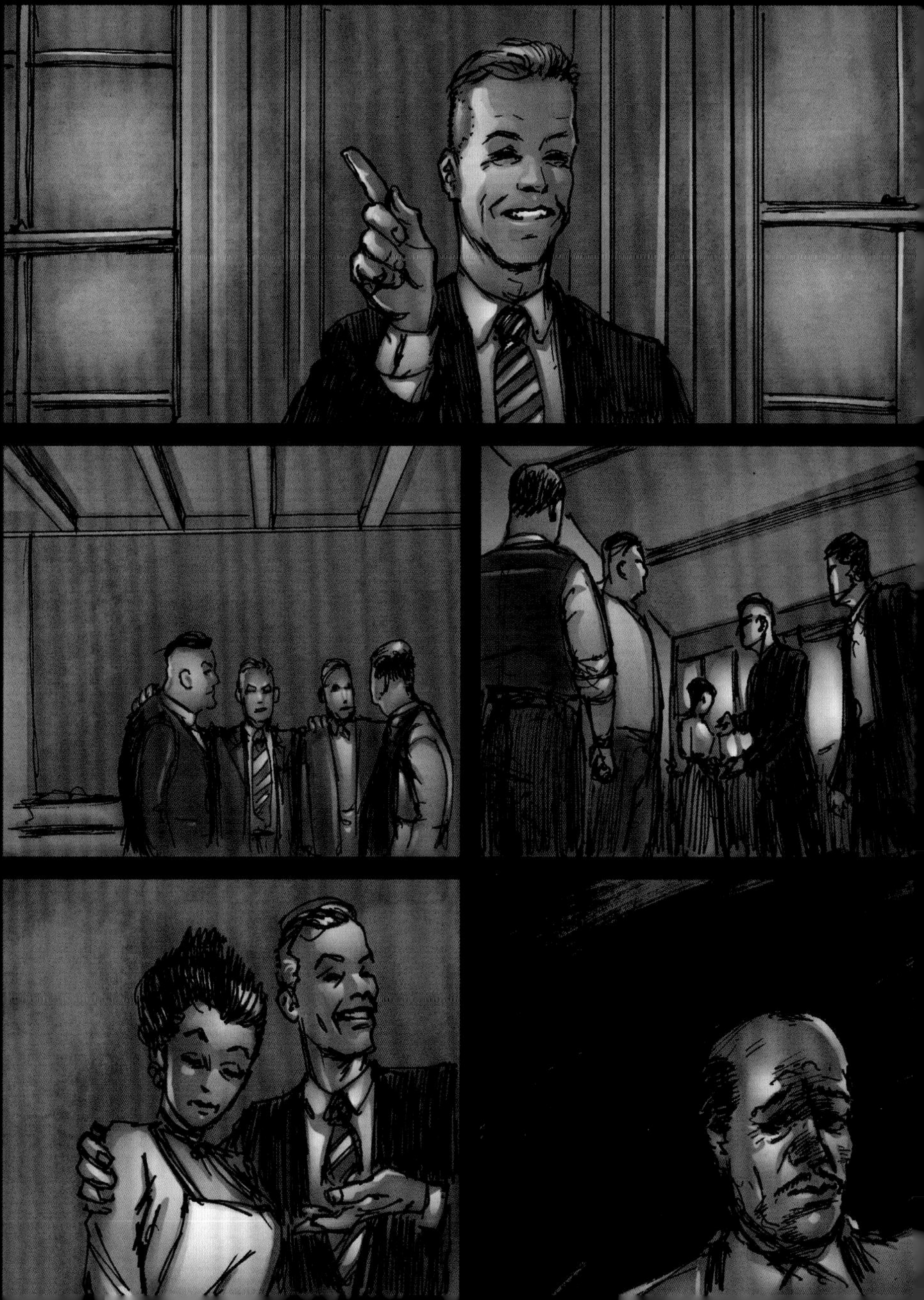

Colors
Page 17
Colors by Peter Pantazis

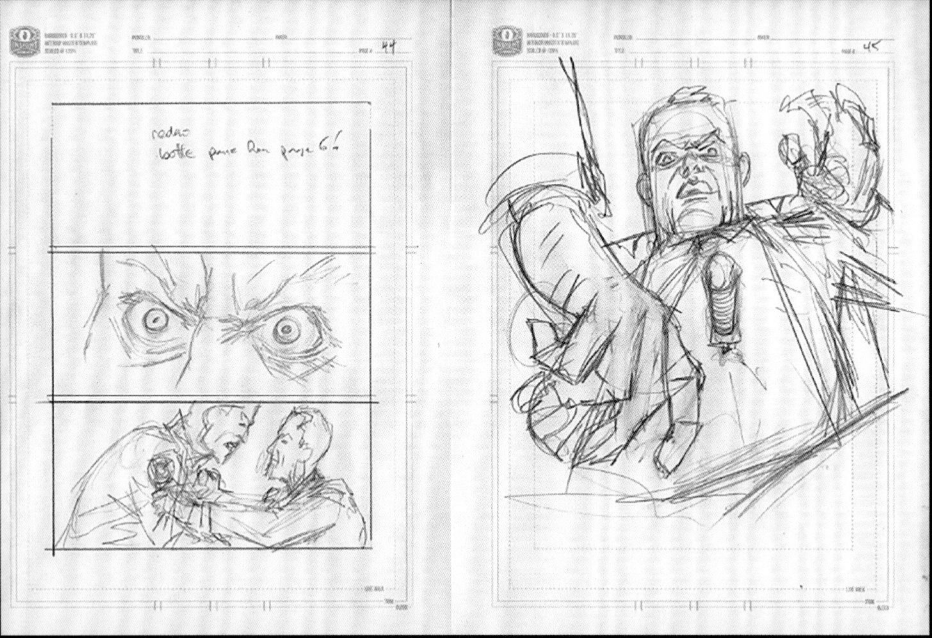

Layout Sketches

Pages 48–49

Art by Richard Pace

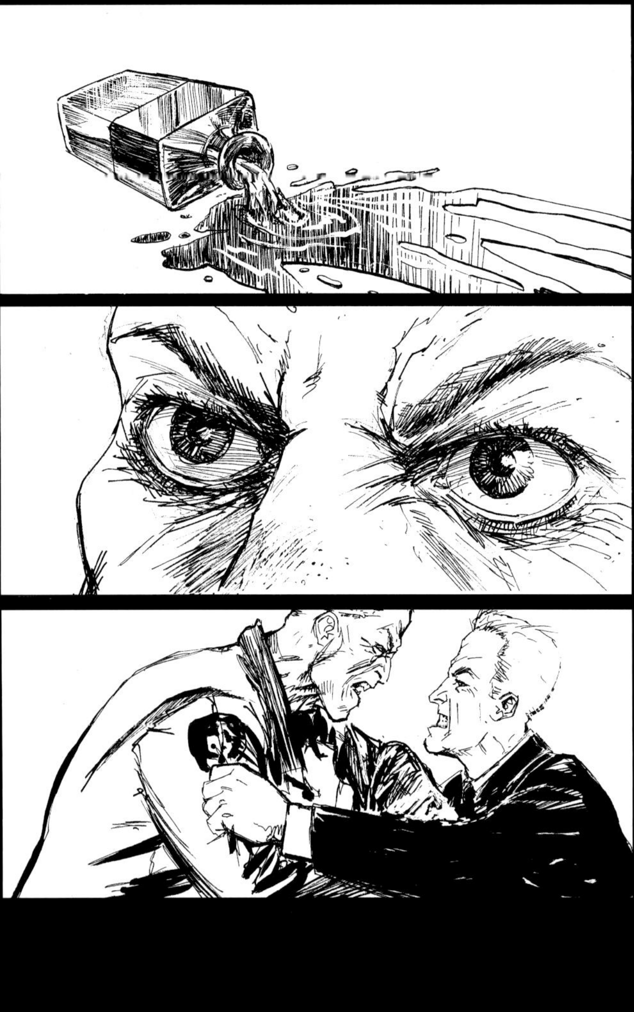

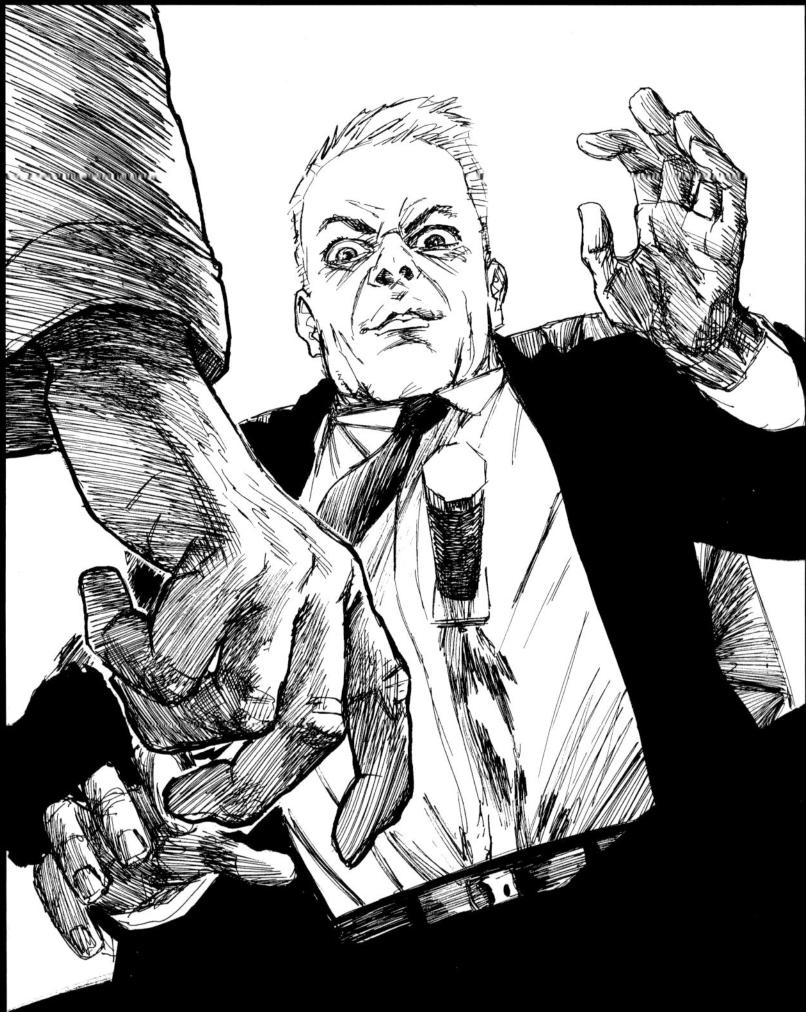

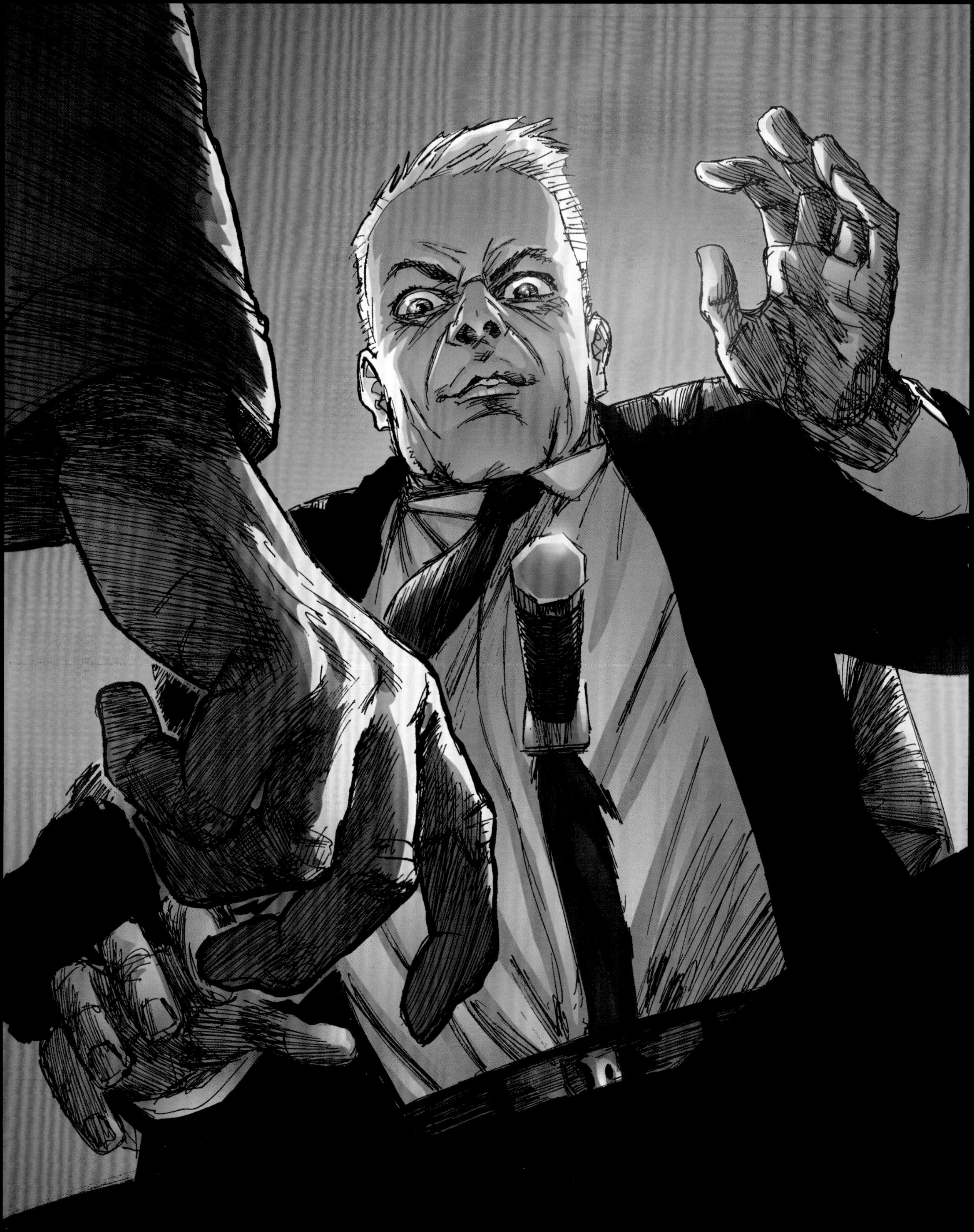

Colors

Page 49

Colors by Peter Pantazis

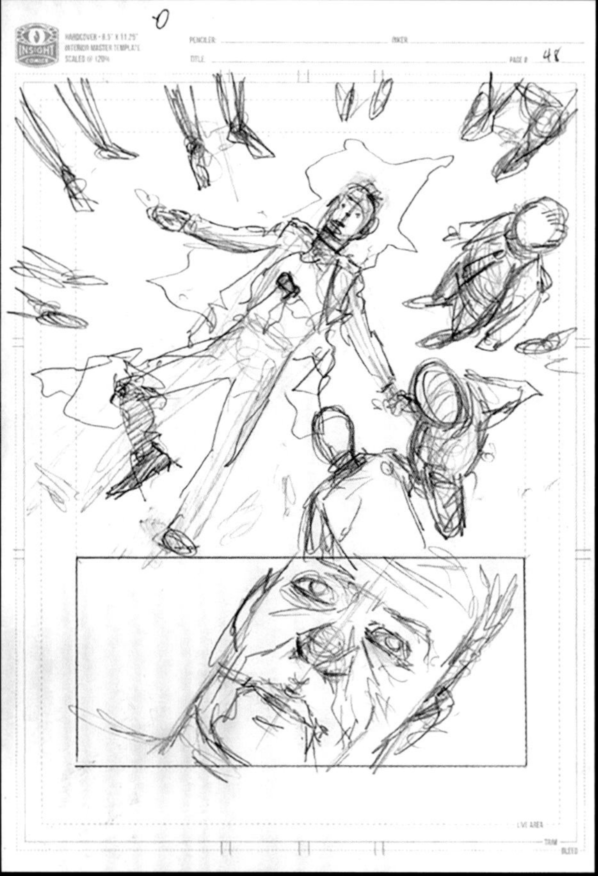

Layout Sketches

Page 52

Art by Richard Pace

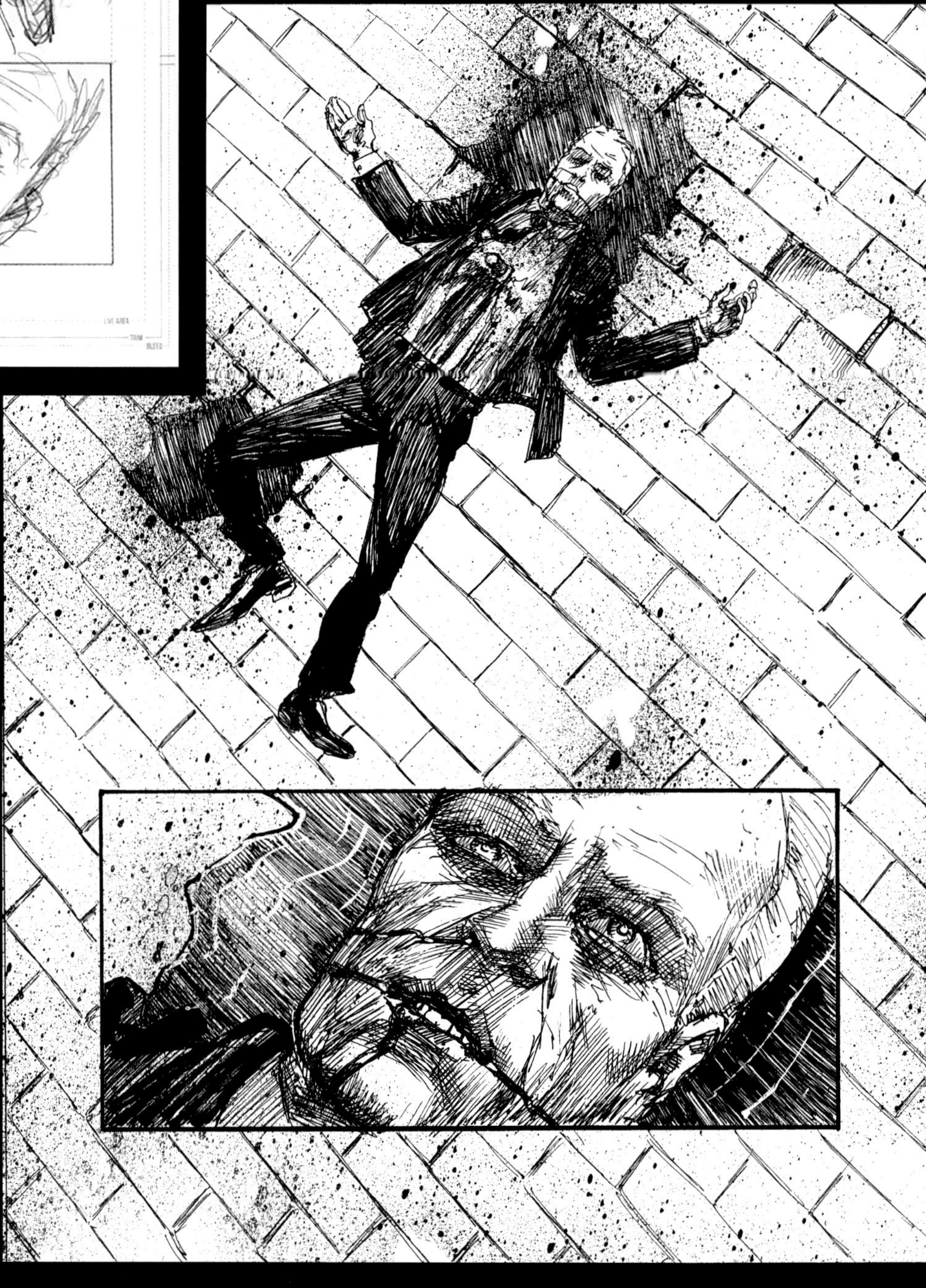

Inks

Page 52

Art by Richard Pace

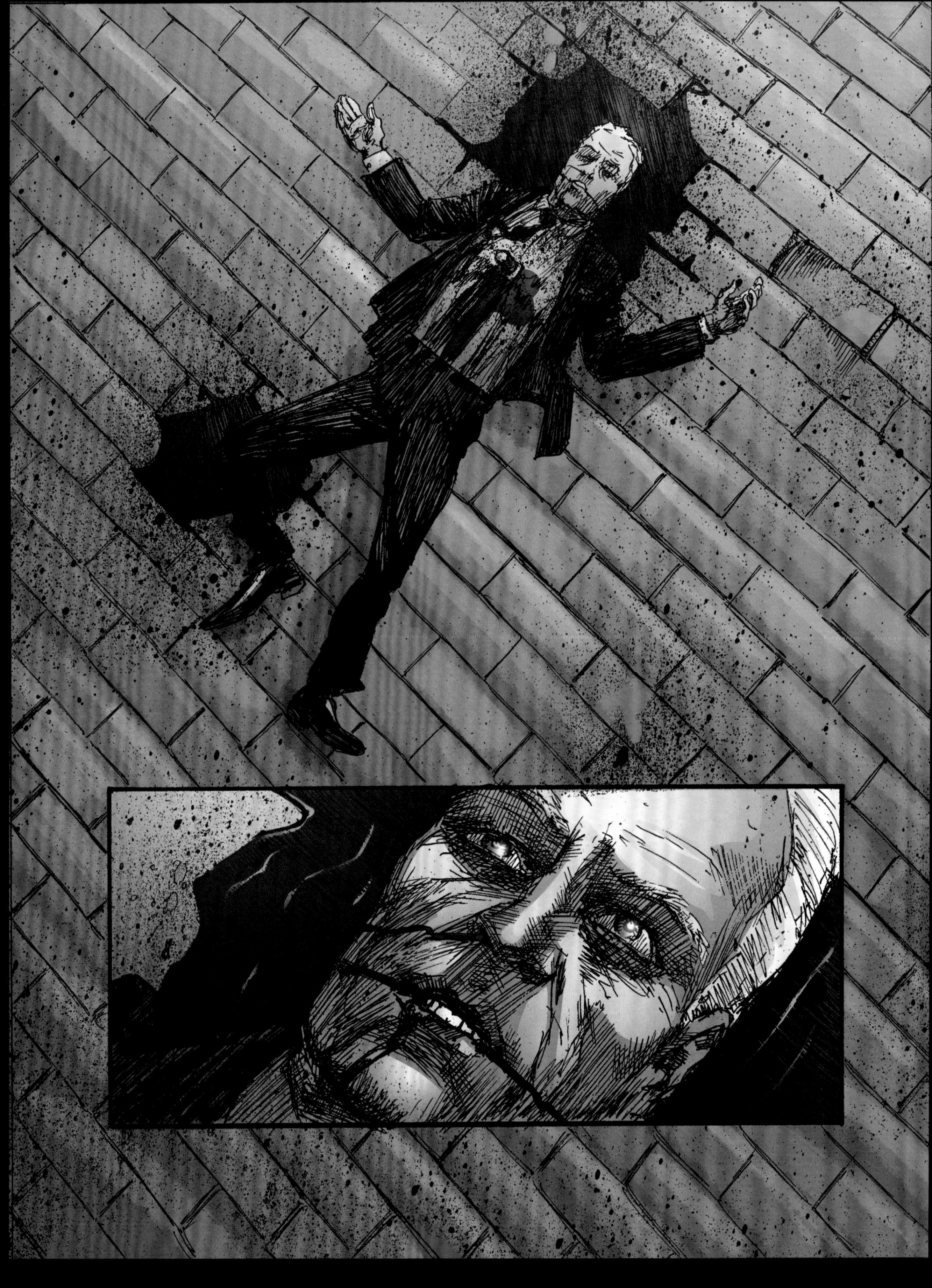

Colors

Page 52

Colors by Peter Pantazis

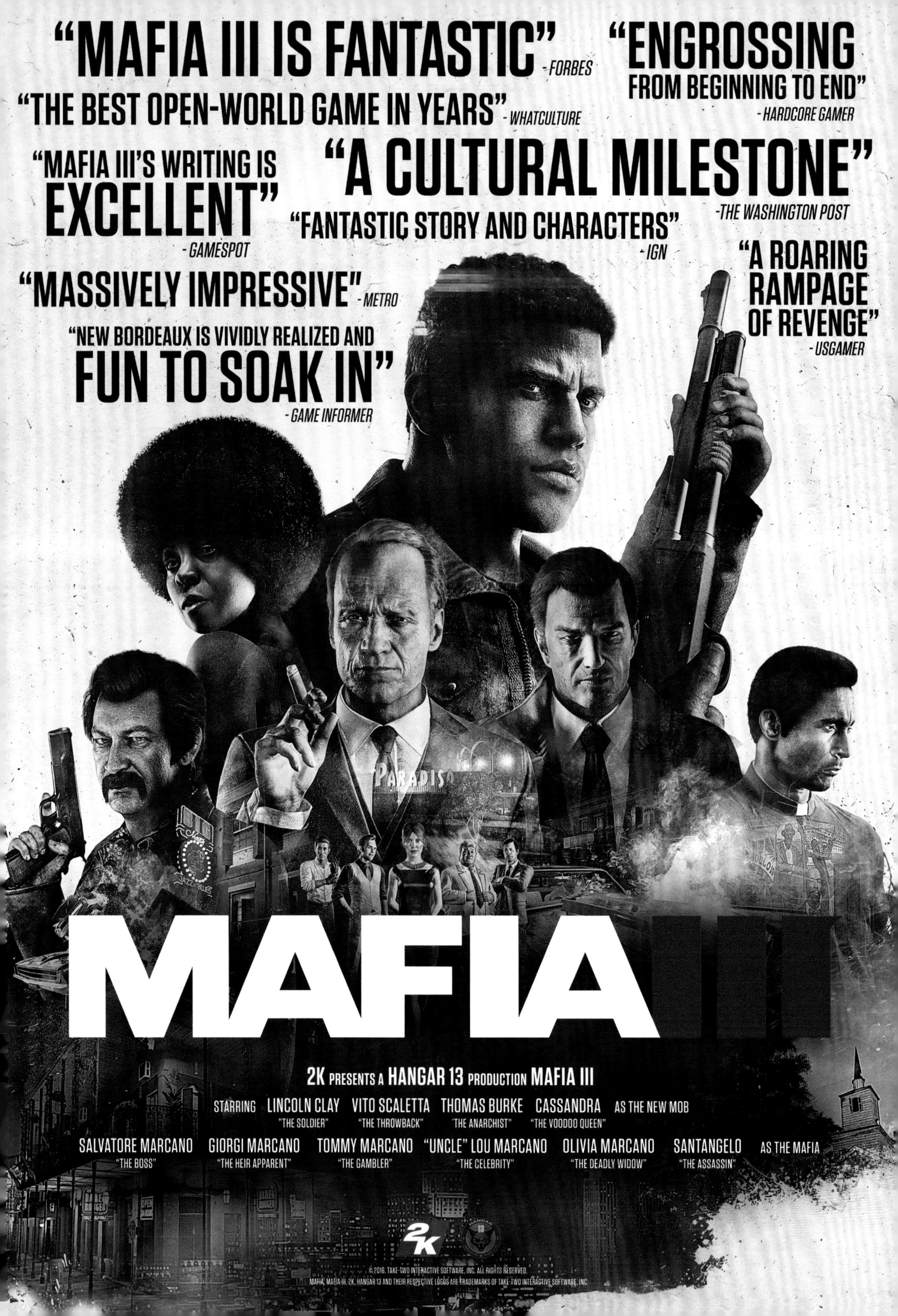

"MAFIA III IS FANTASTIC" - FORBES
"ENGROSSING FROM BEGINNING TO END" - HARDCORE GAMER
"THE BEST OPEN-WORLD GAME IN YEARS" - WHATCULTURE
"MAFIA III'S WRITING IS EXCELLENT" - GAMESPOT
"A CULTURAL MILESTONE" - THE WASHINGTON POST
"FANTASTIC STORY AND CHARACTERS" - IGN
"MASSIVELY IMPRESSIVE" - METRO
"A ROARING RAMPAGE OF REVENGE" - USGAMER
"NEW BORDEAUX IS VIVIDLY REALIZED AND FUN TO SOAK IN" - GAME INFORMER
PARADISO
MAFIA III
2K PRESENTS A HANGAR 13 PRODUCTION MAFIA III
STARRING LINCOLN CLAY "THE SOLDIER" VITO SCALETTA "THE THROWBACK" THOMAS BURKE "THE ANARCHIST" CASSANDRA "THE VOODOO QUEEN" AS THE NEW MOB
SALVATORE MARCANO "THE BOSS" GIORGI MARCANO "THE HEIR APPARENT" TOMMY MARCANO "THE GAMBLER" "UNCLE" LOU MARCANO "THE CELEBRITY" OLIVIA MARCANO "THE DEADLY WIDOW" SANTANGELO "THE ASSASSIN" AS THE MAFIA
2K
HANGAR 13
© 2016. TAKE-TWO INTERACTIVE SOFTWARE, INC. ALL RIGHTS RESERVED.
MAFIA, MAFIA III, 2K, HANGAR 13 AND THEIR RESPECTIVE LOGOS ARE TRADEMARKS OF TAKE-TWO INTERACTIVE SOFTWARE, INC.

Also Available

THE ART OF
MAFIA

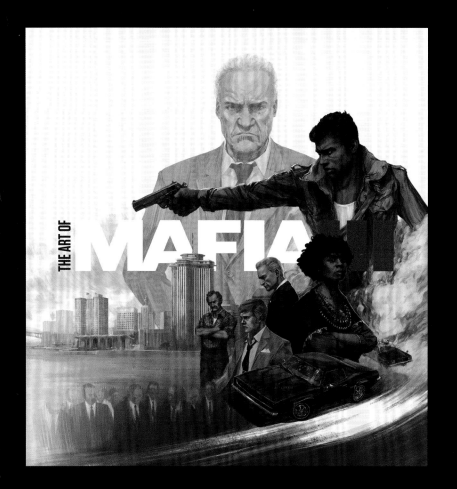

In *Mafia III,* game developer 2K has players join Lincoln Clay as he builds his own criminal organization in 1968 New Bordeaux. This deluxe art book collects the striking art behind *Mafia III,* offering exclusive explorations of the characters and locations that bring the world of the game to life. Complete with commentary from art director Dave Smith, *The Art of Mafia III* offers an incredible behind-the-scenes look at this landmark title.

MAFIA
PLAIN OF JARS
JEFF MARIOTTE AND
MARSHELLA ROCKWELL

This novel, modeled in the style of detective "pulp" novels from the 1960s, expands upon the world of 1968 New Bordeaux, Louisiana, a city ruled by organized crime and corrupt officials as depicted in the hit videogame *Mafia III*. Featuring characters and locations from the game, and a brand new original storyline full of intrigue, suspense, passion, and violence, *Mafia III: Plain of Jars* is a great read for fans of the game and crime genre hounds looking for another intriguing story to delve into.

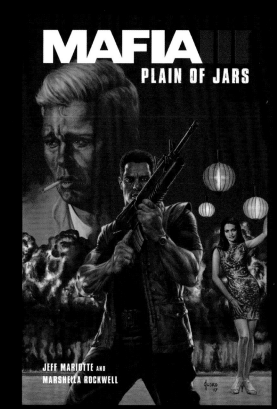

An Imprint of Insight Editions
PO Box 3088
San Rafael, CA 94912
www.insighteditions.com

Find us on Facebook: www.facebook.com/InsightEditions
Follow us on Twitter: @insighteditions
Follow us on Instagram: Insight_Comics

Published by Insight Comics, an imprint of Insight Editions, San Rafael, California, in 2018.

Library of Congress Cataloging-in-Publication Data available.

ISBN: 978-1-60887-998-4

Publisher: Raoul Goff
Associate Publisher: Vanessa Lopez
Art Director: Chrissy Kwasnik
Executive Editor: Mark Irwin
Managing Editor: Alan Kaplan
Editorial Assistants: Hilary VandenBroek and Holly Fisher
Senior Production Editor: Elaine Ou
Production Manager: Greg Steffen

ROOTS of PEACE REPLANTED PAPER

Insight Editions, in association with Roots of Peace, will plant two trees for each tree used in the manufacturing of this book. Roots of Peace is an internationally renowned humanitarian organization dedicated to eradicating land mines worldwide and converting war-torn lands into productive farms and wildlife habitats. Roots of Peace will plant two million fruit and nut trees in Afghanistan and provide farmers there with the skills and support necessary for sustainable land use.

Manufactured in China by Insight Editions

10 9 8 7 6 5 4 3 2 1